NW

JL

RECIPES FROM HISTORIC
AMERICA

RECIPES FROM HISTORIC AMERICA

COOKING & TRAVELING WITH AMERICA'S FINEST HOTELS

LINDA & STEVE BAUER

BRIGHT SKY PRESS

To Mike and Chris.
Thanks for the memories ... so far.

BRIGHT SKY PRESS

Box 416
Albany, Texas 76430

10   9   8   7   6   5   4   3   2   1

Library of Congress Cataloging-in-Publication Data

Bauer, Linda.
Recipes from historic America : cooking and traveling with America's
finest hotels / Linda & Steve Bauer.
p. cm.
ISBN-13: 978-1-931721-68-4 (hardcover : alk. paper)
1. Cookery, American. 2. Hotels—United States—Guidebooks. 3. Historic
buildings—United States—Guidebooks. I. Bauer, Steve, 1943– II. Title.

TX715.B349228 2006
641.5973—dc22

2006040560

For front and divider pages photo captions, please see page 208.

Book and cover design by Isabel Lasater Hernandez
Edited by Kristine Krueger

Printed in China through Asia Pacific Offset

Contents

Introduction

Fed up with fast food? Bored with the chain restaurant scene? Why not please your palate, nourish your mind and enjoy a bit of unique American history at the same time? From a windswept beach experience ... to a magnificent mansion on a wooded hillside ... to a serene lake setting ... to a soaring downtown high-rise, the rich fabric of America has been preserved and is available to diners in some of the best restaurants in the country.

Recipes from Historic America points the way to these grand establishments, combining stories from the past with up-to-date information and appetizing recipes.

The lure of travel in America grows with every problem abroad. The United States is increasingly becoming a tourist destination for Americans reluctant to go outside its borders, as well as for foreigners attracted to that wonderful place they see often in the media and can now afford to visit. The hustle and bustle of the big cities, the majesty of the mountains, the expanse of the plains and the mystery of the "Wild West" combine to make America unique among the world's travel destinations.

In 2004, travel and tourism accounted for nearly a trillion dollars of the nation's economy, according to the Bureau of Economic Analysis, an agency of the U.S. Department of Commerce. And expenditures on food services were approximately $200 billion of that amount. "Dining out" is a regular pastime for Americans ... and tourists from around the globe, eager to try something new, add to the crowds.

An attitude of western hospitality is evident throughout the USA and especially at the historic restaurants, where generations have lovingly passed down the properties. They want to share their stories with patrons and are eager to serve their often award-winning cuisine, from simple barbecue to elegant fare.

In our 20 years of writing international food and travel columns, we have been amazed at the way an excellent restaurant with a special atmosphere enhances any dining experience or vacation. A historic venue combined with interesting cuisine—ethnic, regional, classic or family-style—creates a memorable dining adventure. How exciting it is to dine at an establishment where U.S. presidents, Hollywood and sports stars, authors and business tycoons have also enjoyed a delicious meal.

This volume is an effort to help visitors, locals and gourmands find some of the finest food at some of the most interesting restaurants in the country. Pictures of the property, a bit of history and contact information are included, along with some of the popular recipes from their menus. So you can capture the flavor of these places without ever leaving home.

It's more likely that you'll want to re-create a dish after a visit—because once you've read about these intriguing spots, you'll be ready to pack your bags. Bon Appétit ... and Bon Voyage!

THE NORTHEAST

New York and New England—Connecticut, Maine, Massachusetts, New Hampshire, Rhode Island and Vermont. The oldest region of the country, the Northeast is home to the largest city in the nation (New York City) and the smallest state (Rhode Island). Dating back to the Pilgrims, the establishment of permanent colonies in North America and the birth of the nation, the area is rich with history and cultural and economic opportunities. It's a popular tourist destination.

Chatham Bars Inn

Chatham Bars Inn

297 Shore Road

Chatham, Massachusetts

02633

(508) 945-0096

(800) 527-4884

www.chathambarsinn.com

Chatham Bars Inn has been New England's premier oceanfront resort and a renowned Cape Cod landmark since 1914. The turn-of-the-century main inn sits gracefully atop a rise overlooking Pleasant Bay and the Atlantic Ocean, while luxurious Cape-style cottages dot the surrounding landscape.

The property on which Chatham Bars Inn and its golf course are located was originally part of the Sears family homestead in the 1700s. The last Sears member to own and operate the farmland was the Honorable Richard Sears, known in his day as "Squire Sears."

Richard was born in Chatham in 1749. When he was 11, his father passed away and he moved with his mother to Boston after she remarried. At the age of 13, Richard moved back to Chatham and lived under the care of General Joseph Otis. When Richard came of adult age, he became the largest real estate owner in Chatham. Along with running the farm, Richard also owned a variety store and was engaged in saltworks.

Sears held many prominent positions throughout his life. He was coroner in 1781, justice of the court and justice of the peace in 1814. He was the elected town representative to the General Court 11 times between 1780 and 1814. He also served as senator, town clerk, treasurer and lieutenant of the town militia in the Revolutionary War. He died in 1839 at the age of 90.

In 1912, Charles Ashley Hardy began to purchase the land where the hotel and golf course are now located with the hope of opening a hunting lodge for Boston vacationers. When Chatham Bars Inn opened on June 14, 1914, it catered to the hunting crowd. Nat A. Eldredge, the first general manager of Chatham Bars Inn, led guests on foxhunts in the Chatham and Monomoy Island area. They also hunted quail, waterfowl and plover.

The increase of recreational hunting, and commercial hunting of waterfowl and shorebirds for markets and millinery trade, threatened the extinction of some bird populations. The Federal Migratory Bird Treaty was passed in 1916, putting an end to the hunting of fowl. The foxhunts continued into the 1930s.

The Main Inn and nine of the cottages were designed and built by Boston architect Harvey Bailey Alden. William H. Cox was the architect of the other nine original cottages. The style was typical of local resort architecture of the day.

The cuisine was considered "the best of New England cooking with special attention to seafood ... offering clean dairy milk, cream and butter, and fruit and vegetables from model Cape Cod farms." For many years, the vegetables were grown in the hotel gardens where Greensleeves Nursery now resides. An early dinner menu reveals a variety of local shellfish and game delicacies, as well as two curious New England dishes, Yorkshire Buck and Yarmouth Bloaters.

Famous individuals who have stayed at the inn include Henry Ford, Henry

Morganthau, William Rockefeller and the Dutch Royal Family, who spent part of their World War II exile at Chatham Bars Inn.

When Charles Hardy died in 1929, after a hunting accident, the management of the hotel was continued by the Chatham Associates, a trust company incorporated in January 1916 by Hardy and his associates. The resort continued to maintain the gracious style and attentive service it had become known for.

In 1953, the Associates of the Chatham Trust sold the hotel and property to E.R. McMullen, a longtime summer resident. McMullen sold Chatham Bars Inn to William Langelier in 1986–87. Langelier and his partner, Alan Green, invested over $2 million in capital improvements and were the first owners to keep the hotel open year-round.

Great American Life Insurance Company purchased the resort in 1994. At that time, a multimillion-dollar restoration project commenced and continues today. Chatham Bars Inn is recognized as a destination of significant value by the National Trust for Historic Preservation and Historic Hotels of America.

The 205 guestrooms and suites combine the best of past and present in everything from fireplaces and exquisite hand-painted furniture to nightly turndown service and wireless Internet access.

Amenities include a quarter mile of private sandy beach, outdoor pool, complimentary children's program, four award-winning restaurants, beachside clambakes and barbecues, seven impressive meeting rooms, tennis courts, spa and adjacent golf—all on 25 splendid acres. It's a short stroll to the charming village of Chatham, which has many historic sites, unique shops and galleries.

CHATHAM BARS INN CLAM CHOWDER

Serves 12

¹/₄ pound unsalted butter

1 cup chopped Spanish onion

1 cup chopped celery

¹/₂ to ³/₄ cup all-purpose flour

3 cups chopped clams

4 bottles (8 ounces *each*) clam juice

2¹/₂ ounces salt pork, scored

1 teaspoon clam base *or* 2 medium clam
  bouillon cubes

2 cups diced potatoes, cooked

1 pint half-and-half cream, warmed

Salt and pepper to taste

In a large saucepan or soup pot, melt the butter; sauté onion and celery until translucent. Stir in flour; cook for 5 minutes. Drain clams, reserving juice; add juice to the bottled clam juice. Set clams aside. Add clam juice to the saucepan and whisk until smooth. Add salt pork, clam base and chopped clams; cook for 20 minutes.

Add cooked potatoes. Let stand for 20 minutes. Remove and discard salt pork. Stir in cream. Season with salt and pepper.

CHOCOLATE PEANUT BUTTER CRUNCH CAKE

WITH PEANUT BRITTLE AND CHOCOLATE SAUCE

$1/2$ ounce dark cocoa powder

6 tablespoons boiling water

4 tablespoons butter, softened

5 ounces brown sugar

1 egg

1 teaspoon vanilla extract

$2 1/2$ ounces all-purpose flour

1 teaspoon baking soda

$1/4$ teaspoon salt

5 tablespoons sour cream

Filling

4 ounces bittersweet chocolate, chopped

$4 1/2$ ounces creamy peanut butter

4 ounces feuilletine (crushed wafer cookies)
  or 1.3 ounces Rice Krispies

Chocolate Mousse

7 ounces bittersweet chocolate, chopped

2 tablespoons butter

1 cup heavy whipping cream

2 eggs

$4 1/2$ ounces sugar

Peanut Butter Mousse

1 cup heavy whipping cream

1 package (8 ounces) cream cheese, softened

$4 1/2$ ounces confectioners' sugar

$4 1/2$ ounces creamy peanut butter

Ganache

$3/4$ cup heavy whipping cream

6 ounces bittersweet chocolate, chopped

$2/3$ cup roasted salted peanuts, chopped

Peanut Brittle

$1/2$ pound butter

1 tablespoon light corn syrup

1 tablespoon water

8 ounces sugar

5 ounces roasted salted peanuts

Chocolate Sauce

1 tablespoon water

3 tablespoons butter

2 ounces sugar

3 tablespoons light corn syrup

$1/2$ ounce bittersweet chocolate, chopped

$1/2$ ounce dark cocoa powder

For the cake, in a small bowl, whisk cocoa powder and boiling water; set aside. In a mixing bowl, cream butter and brown sugar until fluffy. Beat in egg and vanilla. Combine flour, baking soda and salt; add to creamed mixture. Add cocoa mixture and sour cream. (Scrape sides of bowl well between each addition.)

Pour into a parchment paper-lined 9-inch round baking pan. Bake at 350° for 20 minutes. Cool and chill. Trim top of cake. Place in a 9-inch x 2½-inch cake ring. For filling, melt chocolate and peanut butter; fold in feuilletine. Spread over cake. Freeze.

For chocolate mousse, melt chocolate and butter; set aside. Whip heavy cream until soft; chill. In a mixing bowl over a double boiler, whisk eggs and sugar until warm to the touch and sugar has dissolved. Place on mixer and whip until thick and light in color, about 5 minutes. By hand, whisk in melted chocolate mixture. Fold in

whipped cream. Spread over filling. Freeze for 20 minutes.

For peanut butter mousse, whip cream until soft; set aside. In a mixing bowl, beat cream cheese and confectioners' sugar until soft. Add peanut butter. Fold in whipped cream. Spread over chocolate mousse layer. Freeze for 2½ to 3 hours.

Unmold cake and place on a cardboard circle. Place on a wire rack. For ganache, heat cream; whisk in chocolate. Pour ganache over top of cake and spread onto sides. Coat side of cake with peanuts. Chill.

For brittle, in a saucepan, melt butter over low heat. Add corn syrup, water and sugar. Cook, stirring occasionally, until mixture reaches hard-crack stage (290°) and is amber in color. Remove from the heat; stir in peanuts. Pour onto a parchment paper-lined baking sheet; cool. Break into pieces.

For chocolate sauce, in a saucepan, bring water, butter, sugar and corn syrup to a boil. Whisk in chocolate and cocoa powder; boil for 1 minute. Remove from the heat. Cool to room temperature, about 1½ hours. To serve, use a hot knife to cut cake into 12 slices. Place on plates; drizzle with chocolate sauce. Top with a piece of peanut brittle.

The Fairmont Copley Plaza

The Fairmont Copley Plaza

138 St. James Avenue

Boston, Massachusetts 02116

(617) 267-5300

www.fairmont.com/copley

plaza

Since opening in 1912, the Fairmont Copley Plaza has been a symbol of the city of Boston's rich tradition of culture, history and hospitality. Located in historic Back Bay, the hotel stands alongside the Boston Public Library, Trinity Church and Hancock Tower as the architectural landmarks of Copley Square.

Constructed on the original site of the Museum of Fine Arts, the Fairmont Copley Plaza was designed by Henry Janeway Hardenbergh, who also designed the Plaza in New York. The sister hotels share the same double "P" insignia seen throughout both properties.

The hotel's Oval Room, considered one of the most beautiful rooms in Boston, features a realistic sky and cloud ceiling mural. According to legend, when John Singer Sargent was painting the murals at the Boston Public Library, he'd often come to the hotel and watch the artisans paint the Oval Room's mural while eating lunch. When the artisans asked Sargent to add his touch to the mural, he climbed the scaffolding and painted an angel.

Sargent's angel graced the ceiling for over 30 years until the mural was painted over during renovations in the 1940s. Today, Sargent's angel is the "invisible guardian" of the Oval Room.

Nearly every U.S. President since Taft has stayed at the Fairmont Copley Plaza, along with many foreign dignitaries, royalty and countless celebrities. In addition, the hotel has been featured in several major motion pictures, including The Firm and Blown Away.

Today, the Fairmont Copley Plaza celebrates the completion of a $34 million renovation and restoration, which included all of the guestrooms, suites and meeting space and the addition of Fairmont Gold— an exclusive "hotel within a hotel."

As part of the renovation, the Fairmont Copley Plaza added eight themed suites. The cultural partners for this project are the John F. Kennedy Library and Museum, the Boston Symphony Orchestra, the Museum of Fine Arts, the Boston Public Library, the Museum of Science, the Boston Pops, the Freedom Trail and the Sports Museum. Working with curators and archivists from these organizations, the hotel decorated the suites with artwork and memorabilia designed to give guests an authentic Boston experience.

BUFFALO AU POIVRE

Serves 4

4 tablespoons clarified butter *or* 2 tablespoons
    butter mixed with 2 tablespoons canola oil
4 buffalo tenderloin steaks (10 ounces *each*)
Kosher salt to taste
¹/₂ cup freshly ground black pepper, *divided*
¹/₂ cup Cognac
¹/₂ cup veal stock *or* beef stock mixed with
    hot water
1¹/₂ cups heavy whipping cream

Heat a sauté pan; add butter. Season steaks on each side with salt and ¼ cup pepper, pressing seasonings firmly into the meat. When the butter is hot, cook steaks until golden brown on both sides. Transfer to an ovenproof dish and finish in a 350° oven until meat is cooked to desired temperature.

Discard the drippings from the sauté pan and return to the heat. Add the Cognac and remaining pepper. *Be careful as the Cognac can catch on fire.* Wait until there are no more flames before adding the stock and cream. Cook until the sauce starts to thicken. (Cooking time will vary depending on the quality of the stock.) Reduce the sauce until it coats the back of a spoon. Adjust seasoning if needed; pour over steaks and serve immediately.

OAK ROOM MUSSELS

Serves 10

¹/₄ cup oil
20 cloves garlic, minced
8 pieces finely chopped shallot
10 pounds fresh mussels*
Salt and pepper to taste
2¹/₂ cups white wine
8 pieces seeded diced plum tomato
¹/₂ cup capers
1 cup chopped fresh parsley, *divided*
1¹/₂ pounds cold butter, cubed
Lemon slices *or* wedges

Heat oil in a skillet or sauté pan over high heat; sauté garlic and shallot for 1 minute. Add mussels and season lightly; sauté for 2 minutes. Add wine; cover to allow mussels to steam and open, stirring occasionally. Remove mussels and set aside.

Bring pan juices to a boil. Add tomato, capers and ¾ cup parsley. Simmer until juices are reduced by one-third. Reduce heat to low; whisk in cold butter to thicken and finish the sauce. Season with salt and pepper.

To serve, arrange mussels on plate. Top with sauce. Garnish with lemon and remaining parsley.

*Mussels are cooked per order in the restaurant; batch cooking is recommended for 10 portions.

BOSTON CREAM PIE
FAIRMONT COPLEY PLAZA STYLE

1 1/4 cups unsalted butter, softened

1 cup sugar

1 cup honey

4 eggs

3 cups all-purpose flour

2 teaspoons baking powder

1/2 teaspoon salt

1 cup milk

2 teaspoons vanilla extract

Filling

1 quart milk

1 vanilla bean, split

3 eggs

1/2 pound sugar

2 1/2 ounces cornstarch

Pinch salt

1/2 cup rum, *divided*

In a mixing bowl, cream butter and sugar until light and fluffy. Whip in honey. With mixer at moderate speed, add eggs one at a time, fully incorporating each before adding the next. Sift together the flour, baking powder and salt. Combine milk and vanilla. Alternately add dry ingredients and milk mixture to creamed mixture in two to three batches, finishing with dry ingredients.

Transfer to a buttered and floured 10-inch cake pan. Bake at 350° for 50–60 minutes or until a toothpick comes out clean. Cool on a wire rack for 10–15 minutes before unmolding. Refrigerate for several hours.

For filling, in a saucepan, bring milk and vanilla bean to a boil. In a mixing bowl, beat eggs, sugar, cornstarch and salt until mixture starts to turn white. Slowly pour hot milk into sugar mixture, stirring constantly. Return all to the pan; cook over medium heat, stirring constantly, until mixture thickens and begins to boil. Remove from the heat. Discard vanilla bean. Stir in 1/4 cup rum. Cool completely.

When cake is very cold, cut horizontally into three even layers; brush with remaining rum. Place bottom layer on a cake plate; spread with half of the filling. Top with middle layer and remaining filling. Place top cake layer over filling. Just before serving, cut into wedges and place on dessert plates. Garnish with hot chocolate sauce and white chocolate shavings.

The Garden City Hotel

When multimillionaire Alexander Turney Stewart, "the Merchant Prince of Broadway," purchased 7,000 acres of land approximately 20 miles from New York City, he began planning Garden City and its focal point—a grand hotel that would attract a famous and wealthy clientele from around the world. He succeeded. The Garden City Hotel was pronounced a great success as soon as it opened in 1874.

In 1901, a new Garden City Hotel was erected, complete with a cupola fashioned after the one that sits atop Philadelphia's Independence Hall. Prominent guests—including the Vanderbilts, Astors and Belmonts—stayed at the hotel when visiting Long Island for polo matches, horse races or a new sport at the time, auto racing.

Perhaps the most notable guest was Charles Lindbergh, who dined with friends and family at the hotel the night before his historic flight on May 20, 1927.

From 1910 to '30, the hotel remained at the forefront of Long Island activity, and it became the norm for society's elite to attend the large, fashionable parties held in the hotel's ballroom. However, with the Great Depression, the Gatsby-era excesses of the Garden City Hotel faded, as they did for the entire nation.

After World War II, the community around the hotel began to grow and flourish as a residential suburban village. All the while, the hotel continued to serve as a landmark lodging, attracting vacationers, business executives and world leaders, including a 1959 visit by Presidential-hopeful John F. Kennedy and his wife, Jacqueline, and the recent stays of Senator Hillary Clinton and former Prime Minister Margaret Thatcher.

In the early 1980s, current owner Myron Nelkin built the existing Garden City Hotel. Since then, this world-class, luxury hotel has been guided by the Nelkin family, who continues to uphold the tradition started by Alexander Turney Stewart.

From its post-Civil War beginnings to the Roaring Twenties, the dawn of suburbia to the new millennium, the Garden City Hotel has provided high-quality services and elegant accommodations.

The Garden City Hotel

45 Seventh Street

Garden City, New York 11530

(516) 747-3000

(877) 549-0400

www.gchotel.com

GRILLED WILD STRIPED BASS
WITH CHORIZO AND LITTLENECK CLAMS IN PIPÉRADE

Serves 8

2 ounces mild Spanish chorizo,
    cut into $\frac{1}{2}$-inch slices
1 tablespoon extra virgin olive oil
1 green bell pepper, cut into 1-inch strips
1 red bell pepper, cut into 1-inch strips
$\frac{1}{2}$ Spanish onion, cut into 1-inch strips
2 ripe tomatoes, diced
1 clove garlic, chopped
2 sprigs thyme
Salt and pepper to taste
Red pepper flakes, optional
White wine, optional
12 littleneck clams, washed
4 sprigs flat leaf parsley
2 pounds wild striped bass fillets,
    sliced $\frac{1}{2}$ inch thick
Additional olive oil

In a skillet or saucepan, sauté the chorizo in oil until it starts to brown, about 3 minutes. Remove the chorizo. In the same pan, sauté peppers and onion over medium-low heat until the onion turns translucent. After about 10 minutes, add the chorizo, tomatoes, garlic, thyme, salt, pepper and pepper flakes if desired.

Cover and continue to cook slowly. Add a few tablespoons of white wine if the mixture is too dry. Meanwhile, open the clams on the grill. As soon as they open up, add them to the pipérade with the parsley; mix well.

Rub bass with olive oil; season with salt and pepper. Grill on both sides until done. Place bass on serving plates; top with clams and pipérade.

POTATO GNOCCHI
WITH OYSTERS POACHED IN CHAMPAGNE, SAVOY CABBAGE AND CAVIAR

Serves 4

3 pounds Idaho potatoes

2 cups all-purpose flour

1 egg

1 teaspoon salt

2 cups savoy cabbage, shredded

10 cumin seeds

¼ cup chicken stock

4 tablespoons butter, *divided*

1 tablespoon Pommery mustard

12 oysters with liquid, shucked

2 shallots, chopped

2 cups champagne

1 cup heavy whipping cream, *divided*

½ ounce osetra caviar *or* American paddlefish

Bake potatoes until tender; peel and put through a food mill while still hot. In a bowl, combine the potatoes, flour, egg and salt; mix well. Roll into a ¾-inch-diameter cylinder; cut into 1-inch pieces while gently pinching the center. Freeze. Cook in boiling salted water for 2–3 minutes. Cool immediately in ice water; drain and blot dry with paper towels. Keep refrigerated (or frozen) in a lightly oiled pan.

Blanch cabbage. In a saucepan, sweat cabbage in 2 tablespoons butter with cumin seeds until semisoft. Add chicken stock. Season with salt and pepper. Add mustard. Keep warm.

Warm oysters in liquid with shallots and champagne. Remove oysters. Reduce liquid to ¾ cup. Add ¾ cup cream and remaining butter. Add oysters and gnocchi; heat through. Put cabbage in the center of the bowl; surround with oysters and gnocchi. Whip the remaining cream; fold into sauce. Spoon over oysters. Top each oyster with caviar and serve.

"You cannot truly say you live well unless you eat well."
—Nigella Lawson

The Inn at Sawmill Farm

The Inn at Sawmill Farm

Crosstown Road and

   Route 100

West Dover, Vermont 05356

(802) 464-8131

www.theinnatsawmillfarm.com

Originally known as the Winston Farm, the Inn at Sawmill Farm was built on the site of the first business in West Dover, Vermont—a sawmill. Consisting of over 20 acres, the farm is a stone's throw from Mount Snow.

When the Williams family purchased it in 1967, they intended to use the property as their personal ski retreat. But they decided almost immediately to leave their home and careers in Atlantic City and go into the inn business instead.

The Inn at Sawmill Farm opened with just nine guestrooms, a living room, kitchen and one dining room. Ione Williams ran the kitchen and did the books, while husband Rod took care of the dining room and guests. The family lived in the original farmhouse, which has since been converted into four additional guestrooms. After graduating from college, their son, Brill, joined them and eventually took over the kitchen. He is now the chef-owner.

The years have seen the addition of more dining space and office space. An 18th-century barn with hand-hewn beams and weathered siding became three dining rooms with a cozy copper-topped bar, a large lounge with soaring ceilings and fireplace, and a library/game room where the hayloft used to be. There are two ponds for trout fishing, an outdoor pool, two gazebos and a tennis court.

All 21 guestrooms are different, reflecting Ione's decorating talents. The 10 in the main house are spacious, decorated in rich fabrics and antiques; a few have decks or balconies. Ten rooms with fireplaces, some with Jacuzzis and canopy beds, are in nearby buildings: the Cider House, Farm House, Spring House and Wood Shed.

The last room is actually a one-bedroom suite in the new Carriage House. A barn back in the 18th century, it has been completely renovated, and is decorated with Federal-period antiques, fabrics and custom-upholstered furniture. Utterly private, its tall arched windows and wraparound deck overlook a pond and gardens.

The restaurant is Sawmill's crown jewel. Its exposed beams, chandeliers, sparkling china and impeccable service are classically romantic. The menu features local fare like rabbit, venison and quail. Soups are a specialty of the house, and the desserts are often Mother's home recipes, like ice cream with dark chocolate butternut sauce (the sauce is available for purchase at the inn).

The exceptional wine list has received the *Wine Spectator* Grand Award for the past 11 years. The selection of 1,285 different wines, offering remarkable vintages and labels, is housed in the 28,000-bottle cellar.

Every season is impressive here in the Southern Vermont Valley. In winter, Mount Snow offers skiing and snowboarding on 130 trails ... in summer, hikers can traverse 20 miles of paths and mountain bikers can enjoy 45 miles of trails. A golf school and several professional courses are nearby. Just down the road, fishermen can find the only Orvis-endorsed fly-fishing school in the Northeast.

And, of course, there is fall foliage's grand display during September and October.

Running the inn has continued to be a family affair, with each member's talents flourishing: Rodney is the creator and architect ... Ione the decorator ... Brill the head chef and wine collector ... and daughter Bobbie Dee the administrator.

"We have been growing, not particularly in size because we enjoy the intimacy of a small inn, but we have been active each year with additions and improvements," says Ione. "However, the personality of our inn is still pretty much the same. We still like to think of it as unpretentious, but curiously sophisticated."

VERMONT COUNTRY BREAKFAST

Serves 4

1 cup grade A *or* fancy Vermont maple syrup

2 tablespoons arrowroot

3 tablespoons Grand Marnier

2 Granny Smith apples, peeled and thinly sliced

4 slices Vermont smoked ham

4 eggs

4 English muffin halves

Bring syrup to a boil and remove from the heat immediately (it will overflow as soon as it starts to boil). Mix arrowroot with cold water until it forms a paste; add to the syrup to thicken. Simmer for 3 minutes, then add Grand Marnier. Add apple slices; simmer on low heat. Heat ham slices in the oven or grill slightly until warm. Poach the eggs and toast the English muffins.

Place a muffin half on each plate; top with a poached egg. Place ham slice on the side; pour apple syrup mixture over ham.

SOUR CREAM COFFEE CAKE

Serves 16–20

1 cup butter, softened

3 cups sugar, *divided*

4 eggs

3 cups all-purpose flour

2 teaspoons baking soda

2 cups sour cream

2 teaspoons vanilla extract

5 tablespoons flaked coconut

5 tablespoons walnut pieces

2 teaspoons cinnamon

In a mixing bowl, beat butter and 2 cups sugar. Beat in eggs, one at a time. Sift flour and baking soda; add to egg mixture alternately with sour cream, beginning and ending with flour. Add vanilla. In another bowl, combine the coconut, walnuts, cinnamon and remaining sugar.

Lightly butter and flour a 13-inch x 9-inch x 2-inch baking pan. Pour batter into pan; top with coconut mixture and swirl into batter with a knife. Bake at 350° for 1 hour or until a toothpick comes out clean.

SHRIMP IN BEER BATTER

Serves 4

Dipping Sauce

1 tablespoon prepared horseradish

1 teaspoon powdered ginger

Juice of 2 oranges

Juice of 1 lemon

1 cup marmalade

Batter

1 1/2 cups all-purpose flour

1 tablespoon paprika

1 teaspoon sea salt

1 teaspoon freshly cracked black pepper

1 bottle (12 ounces) beer

Shrimp

12 raw shrimp, peeled and deveined

1/2 cup all-purpose flour

1/2 teaspoon salt

1/2 teaspoon pepper

2 cups sliced blanched almonds

Vegetable oil for frying

In a bowl, make a paste of the horseradish and ginger. Slowly stir in the orange and lemon juices until smooth. Add the marmalade; mix well. Refrigerate until chilled before serving.

Combine the batter ingredients in a bowl; mix until completely smooth and free of lumps. Pat the shrimp dry. Combine the flour, salt and pepper; toss with the shrimp. Holding each shrimp by the tail, dip into batter and gently shake off excess. Coat shrimp with almonds.

Heat oil in a deep fryer; fry shrimp, a few at a time, until golden brown, about 2–3 minutes. Do not crowd the fryer. Drain on paper towels and keep warm.

To serve, arrange three shrimp per person on a small plate with the dipping sauce. Good with champagne!

The Mount Washington Hotel & Resort

The Mount Washington
   Hotel & Resort
Route 302
Bretton Woods,
   New Hampshire 03575
(603) 278-1000
(800) 314-1752
www.mtwashington.com

Situated in scenic Bretton Woods is a masterpiece of Spanish Renaissance architecture—the Mount Washington Hotel, built by industrialist Joseph Stickney, a New Hampshire native who made his fortune in coal mining and the Pennsylvania Railroad. Ground was broken in 1900 and construction completed in 1902 with the help of 250 Italian craftsmen. On July 28 of that year, the doors of this grand hotel opened to the public.

Bretton Woods is part of a land grant made in 1772 by Royal Governor John Wentworth. The area was named after Bretton Hall, Wentworth's ancestral home in Yorkshire, England.

The most luxurious hotel of its day, the Mount Washington catered to wealthy guests from Boston, New York and Philadelphia. As many as 50 trains a day stopped at Bretton Woods' three railroad stations. One of these stations, Fabyan's, is now one of the resort's dining establishments.

Over the years, the hotel has been host to countless celebrities, including Winston Churchill, Thomas Edison, Babe Ruth and three Presidents.

In 1944, it was the site of the Bretton Woods International Monetary Conference. Delegates from 44 nations convened there, establishing the World Bank and International Monetary Fund, setting the gold standard at $35 an ounce and designating the U.S.

dollar as the backbone of international exchange. The formal documents were signed in the Gold Room, located off the hotel's lobby and now preserved as a historic site.

In 1978, the Mount Washington Hotel was listed on the National Register of Historic Places. In 1986, the hotel and the Bretton Arms Country Inn (also located on the property) were designated as National Historic Landmarks. In 1991, a group of local entrepreneurs joined forces to preserve the historic property. Today, this grande dame has been restored to its original grandeur.

Situated in the heart of the White Mountain National Forest, the 2,000-acre private resort can accommodate groups of up to 1,000 people year-round. Located just 20 minutes east of Interstate 93 and 30 minutes west of Route 16, the resort is easily accessible from all directions. A helicopter landing pad is available on the grounds.

Nestled in the Ammonoosuc River Valley and ringed by mountain ranges, the area is noted for crisp, clean air, spectacular scenery and endless outdoor recreation. Just 3 miles north of Crawford Notch, the resort offers breathtaking views dominated by Mount Washington, the highest peak in the Northeast. Mount Washington is famous for its unique alpine flora and a view described by P.T. Barnum as "the second greatest show on Earth."

BLUE CHEESE AND SPICED WALNUT TERRINE

Yields approximately 4 cups

1 teaspoon ground cumin

1/2 teaspoon salt

1/4 teaspoon ground cardamom

1/4 teaspoon ground black pepper

1 tablespoon olive oil

1 cup walnuts

3 tablespoons sugar

1 pound Maytag blue cheese, crumbled, *divided*

2 1/2 ounces fresh chèvre

2 1/2 ounces cream cheese, room temperature

1/4 pound butter, room temperature

2 tablespoons brandy

1/2 cup minced scallions

2 tablespoons minced parsley

2 tablespoons minced chives

Combine the cumin, salt, cardamom and pepper; set aside. Heat oil in a heavy skillet over medium heat. Add walnuts and sauté until light brown. Sprinkle with sugar; sauté until sugar melts and turns light amber. Remove from the heat; toss nuts with spice mixture. Cool.

In a food processor, combine 1/2 pound blue cheese, chèvre, cream cheese and butter; purée until smooth. Transfer to a bowl; fold in brandy and scallions. Mix parsley and chives in a separate bowl.

Oil a skinny terrine mold and line with plastic wrap. Pipe a third of the cheese mixture into the bottom of mold and spread out evenly. Sprinkle with a third of the remaining blue cheese, a third of the spiced nuts and a third of the parsley-chive mixture. Repeat layers twice. Cover and refrigerate overnight.

PAN-BRAISED HENS
WITH NEW POTATOES AND RED WINE SAUCE

Serves 4

1¼ pounds mirepoix, finely chopped

4 bay leaves, crushed

½ ounce black peppercorns, crushed

½ bunch parsley, coarsely chopped (stems and all)

Kosher salt as needed

½ bottle (750ml) red wine

4 Cornish game hens

Flour and olive oil as needed

2 quarts chicken stock

2 pounds new potatoes

6 tablespoons butter

24 pearl onions

16 white mushrooms, quartered

2 ounces pancetta, diced

2 leeks (white portion only), bias-cut into
    2-inch pieces

Thyme and celery leaves for garnish

In a large container, combine the mirepoix, bay leaves, peppercorns, parsley, salt and wine; mix well. Add game hens. Cover and refrigerate overnight.

Remove chicken from marinade. Strain and reserve marinade. Dust chicken with flour and brown in olive oil; remove. Add reserved marinade to the pan; bring to a rolling boil and reduce by half. Add the stock and hens; reduce heat to a simmer. Cover with buttered parchment paper. Finish in a 325° oven until chicken is tender but not falling apart.

Meanwhile, cook the potatoes until tender; drain and mash with olive oil. Remove chicken and keep warm. Skim and reduce cooking juices; strain. Whisk in butter; keep warm. In a large skillet or pan, heat olive oil. Add pearl onions, mushrooms, pancetta and leeks; allow to brown. Splash with a small amount of sauce.

To serve, place a spoonful of mashed potatoes in the middle of plate. Spoon some vegetables in front of potatoes. Prop a game hen against the potatoes. Drizzle with sauce and sprinkle with thyme and celery leaves.

"In France, cooking is a serious art form and a national sport."

—Julia Child

The Waldorf=Astoria

The Waldorf=Astoria®

301 Park Avenue

New York, New York 10022

(212) 355-3000

(800) 925-3673

www.waldorfastoria.com

On March 24, 1893, millionaire William Waldorf Astor opened the 13-story Waldorf Hotel on the site of his former mansion, at Fifth Avenue at 33rd Street. Built by renowned architect Henry Janeway Hardenbergh, the Waldorf was the embodiment of Astor's vision of a grand hotel, complete with electricity throughout and private bathrooms in many guest chambers.

Four years later, the 17-story Astoria Hotel was erected on an adjacent site by Waldorf's cousin John Jacob Astor IV. The corridor built to connect the two buildings became an enduring symbol of the combined hotels. It is represented by the equal sign in the Waldorf=Astoria name.

In 1929, after decades of hosting distinguished visitors from around the world, a decision was made to tear down the original Waldorf=Astoria in order to erect the Empire State Building and pave the way for a reincarnation 15 blocks north on Park Avenue.

When it opened on October 1, 1931, the Waldorf=Astoria was the world's largest and tallest hotel, a veritable city-within-a-city. President Herbert Hoover himself delivered the radio broadcast message of congratulations upon its opening.

The Empire Room, once the premier entertainment club in New York, helped launch the careers of Diana Ross and Frank Sinatra. The first major film to feature a hotel was *Weekend at the Waldorf,* starring Ginger Rogers. It was the first hotel to be included in the lyrics of a Broadway show— Cole Porter's *You're the Top,* featured in *Anything Goes,* proclaims, "You're a Waldorf Salad."

There is a long list of other "firsts" associated with the Waldorf=Astoria, including the previously mentioned electricity throughout and private bathrooms when it first opened in 1893. Some of the others: abolishing the "Ladies Entrance" ... having assistant managers in the lobby to greet and assist guests with their needs ... introducing room service ... and encouraging people to live permanently in private suites (likely related to the room service introduction).

The hotel became the residence of three five-star generals: Dwight Eisenhower, Douglas MacArthur and Omar Bradley. The five-star insignia is still displayed over the door of the Eisenhower Suite. The Waldorf was recognized as an official New York City Landmark in January 1993.

The Waldorf=Astoria was also the first hotel to give prominence to the Art Deco style in America. The exterior and interior design are acknowledged as masterpieces of this art genre. The Starlight Roof, a jewel of décor and dining, was the first supper club to have a retractable roof.

During recent renovations, totaling in excess of $200 million, many of the hotel's original Art Deco treasures were rediscovered and unveiled, delighting a whole new generation of devoted admirers.

TRUFFLED WALDORF SALAD

This appetizer is currently served from the hotel's room service menu.

Serves 8

2 Granny Smith apples

2 Red Delicious apples

1 fennel bulb

$^1/_3$ cup mayonnaise

$^2/_3$ cup crème fraîche

Juice of $^1/_2$ lemon

6 ounces celeriac, julienned

1 teaspoon black winter truffle, shaved

$^3/_4$ cup walnuts, toasted and coarsely chopped

Core the apples and cut into thick julienne strips. Thinly shave the fennel and place in a bowl of ice water. In a large bowl, combine the mayonnaise, crème fraîche and lemon juice. Add apples, celeriac and truffle; toss gently until well coated.

Dry fennel with a paper towel and arrange in a semicircle in the middle of the plate. Neatly arrange the apple salad in the center of the fennel. Garnish with walnuts.

WALDORF RED VELVET CAKE

1¹/₂ cups sugar

¹/₂ cup shortening

2 eggs

1 teaspoon vanilla extract

2 tablespoons bitter cocoa

¹/₄ cup red food coloring

2¹/₄ cups all-purpose flour

1 teaspoon salt

1 cup buttermilk

1 tablespoon vinegar

1 teaspoon baking soda

In a mixing bowl, beat sugar and shortening until creamy. Beat in eggs and vanilla. Make a paste with the cocoa and food coloring; add to the batter. Sift flour and salt together; add to batter alternately with buttermilk. Mix vinegar and baking soda together; add this immediately as it foams.

Pour into two greased 8-inch cake pans. Bake at 350° for 30–35 minutes or until a toothpick comes out clean. Cool for 10 minutes; remove from pans to wire racks. Frost with cream cheese or vanilla icing.

THOUSAND ISLAND DRESSING

¹/₂ hard-cooked egg

³/₄ cup mayonnaise

¹/₄ cup chili sauce

2 tablespoons ketchup

1¹/₂ tablespoons minced onion

2 teaspoons sweet pickle relish

Freshly ground black pepper

¹/₄ teaspoon kosher salt
  plus more to taste if needed

Push the egg through a sieve or finely chop it; place in a bowl. Whisk in the mayonnaise, chili sauce, ketchup, onion and relish until combined. Season with pepper and salt. Refrigerate until serving.

The White Barn Inn

The White Barn Inn

37 Beach Avenue

Kennebunkport, Maine

04046

(207) 967-2321

www.whitebarninn.com

The attraction of Maine's Kennebunkport region was well recognized by Native Americans, who hunted game in the forests and fished the local waters. In the early 1600s, French and English explorers established trading posts and fishing camps, lured by the success of the Indian population.

At the same time, the white pine and hardwood forests spawned a shipbuilding and shipping community, which flourished for the next 250 years. Trading encompassed the entire eastern seaboard of North America, as well as the West Indies, Europe and the Far East.

Toward the end of the 19th century, as shipbuilding and shipping activities declined in importance, the area benefited from a new force: resort living. Modern conveniences in bustling cities encouraged those with means to escape to the countryside or shore to reconnect with nature.

In 1820, the Forest Hill House was built to accommodate the influx of vacationers. It would eventually be called the White Barn Inn, drawing its name from the ever-present storage facility on the property.

Constructed in typical New England style, the house—along with its outlying property—was purchased in the late 1800s by the Boothby family, who transformed it into an inn catering mainly to a Jewish clientele. They divided the upper floors into guestrooms and added a wraparound porch with Victorian details. The ground floor became spacious living and dining rooms.

When the railroad built a new route and station at Kennebunkport in 1872, Bostonians could suddenly reach the area via a 3-hour train ride. Business boomed as word of mouth and press reports proclaimed the excellent dining available at this extraordinary inn.

Today, the common rooms of the White Barn Inn retain their old-fashioned appeal, with 19th-century-style upholstery and wallpapers, antique portraits, and Oriental carpets laid on hardwood floors. The main floor of the barn has been transformed into a dining room that marries rustic architecture with elegant accoutrements.

Both the rooms in the old house and the more recently constructed cottage-like suites capture the charm of the original inn, which blends easily into the woods surrounding the hilltop property.

The restaurant has a varied menu influenced by local ingredients. Game dishes such as guinea hens, turkey and venison are often garnished with wild mushrooms, New England cranberries and preserved Maine blueberries gathered by local foragers. Lobster, cod and shrimp dishes are regular seaside favorites.

PESTO

Properly stored, pesto will keep without changing color for several days. Transfer the finished pesto to a nonreactive glass or stainless steel container. Pour a thin layer of olive oil over the pesto and cover the container with aluminum foil to keep out light and air.

Makes 1¹/₂ cups

1 bunch fresh basil, stems removed
¹/₂ bunch fresh flat leaf parsley, stems removed
1 clove garlic
³/₄ cup freshly grated Parmesan cheese
1 cup olive oil
¹/₄ cup shelled pistachios
¹/₄ cup pine nuts
¹/₄ cup shelled walnuts
Salt and freshly ground pepper to taste

In a food processor, combine the basil, parsley, garlic, Parmesan cheese and oil; pulse until finely chopped. Add the pistachios, pine nuts and walnuts; chop for a few more seconds, being careful not to overprocess. (The nuts should be chopped to a medium texture but not finely ground.) Season with salt and pepper. Cover and refrigerate until ready to use.

STRAWBERRY JAM

Nothing will make afternoon tea guests feel more special than a bowl filled with just-made jam. This strawberry preserve is easy to make and can be eaten as soon as it cools. Any remaining jam may be canned in glass jars, following proper canning procedures, and stored for up to 6 months.

Makes 1 quart

4 cups ripe strawberries, rinsed, cored and
    quartered
3 cups sugar
Juice of 1 lemon

In a large heavy saucepan, combine the strawberries, sugar and lemon juice. Bring to a boil over medium-high heat. Reduce heat to medium-low. Simmer, uncovered, for 30 minutes or until the mixture is reduced by half, stirring occasionally. Cool and serve, or can in glass jars according to proper canning techniques.

ICED WATERMELON AND BING CHERRY SOUP

The trick to making chilled fruit soups is to keep them light and well balanced in flavor. A soup that's too sweet will overwhelm the palate. The addition of champagne adds an effervescent note. Be sure to serve this as soon as you stir in the chilled champagne.

Serves 4

2 pounds watermelon, peeled, seeded and cubed
1 pound Bing cherries, pitted
1 cup Muscat *or* other white dessert wine
1 cup chilled champagne

In a food processor, purée the watermelon, cherries and wine until smooth. Strain through a fine sieve into a serving bowl or pitcher; cover and refrigerate until chilled. Just before serving, stir in the champagne.

"One of the very nicest things about life is the way we must regularly stop whatever it is we are doing and devote our attention to eating."

–Luciano Pavarotti

THE MID-ATLANTIC

Delaware, Maryland, New Jersey, North Carolina, Pennsylvania, Virginia and West Virginia. From the days of early Colonial settlements, the mid-Atlantic states have contributed heavily to the formation of this great country. Both the nation's first capital (Philadelphia) and its current capital (the District of Columbia) are located here, as well as the homes of a number of our founding fathers. Perhaps one of the most attractive tourist destinations for both citizens and foreigners alike is the historic city of Washington, D.C.

Antrim 1844 Country House Hotel

Antrim 1844

30 Trevanion Road

Taneytown, Maryland 21787

(410) 756-6812

(800) 858-1844

www.antrim1844.com

An immigrant from County Antrim, Ireland, Colonel Andrew Ege acquired 2,500 acres in Taneytown, Maryland, turning it into a thriving plantation with a variety of crops and orchards, much the same as Carroll County farmers produce today. Ege, who'd made his fortune as an inventor and farmer, built a country house on the property in 1844, named it after his wife's birthplace and gave it to their daughter as a wedding gift.

The surrounding outbuildings—the Post House, Ice House, Summer Kitchen, Brick Kitchen, Servants' Wing, Smokehouse, Barn, Spring House, Brick Outhouses and Carriage House—are original to the property.

Unfortunately, shortly after Antrim was completed, Col. Ege went bankrupt, and the property was put up for auction in 1873. George Washington Clabaugh bought Antrim, and it remained in his family for over a century. When he passed away in 1916, he left it to his niece, Helen Clabaugh Lamberton.

Family members living in Washington, D.C., summered at Antrim and used it periodically for family functions (some older residents of Taneytown still remember these parties), but the house remained virtually unoccupied except for an occasional renter in the Servants' Wing and Carriage House. At the time, there was little plumbing and less electricity.

In 1961, the Lambertons sold the house and what remained of the land to George Crouse of Taneytown, who never lived on the property, but had it registered as a National Historic Trust Property.

Current owners Richard and Dorothy Mollett lived for a time in the Smith House, originally a farmhouse built about a mile away from Antrim in 1860. After having it moved to the property to save it from destruction, they restored it for their own residence. It was later turned into additional guest suites.

Nine guestrooms in the manor have been restored, while 20 additional suites and guestrooms are located in the uniquely restored outbuildings. They have a European ambience, with imported antiques and authentic wall hangings, rich fabrics, ornate gilt-frame mirrors, and handsome portraits illuminated by candelabras.

Afternoon tea is served in the Drawing Rooms. In the evenings, guests can enjoy the sunset over the Catoctin Mountains while hors d'oeuvres are passed. The award-winning Smokehouse Restaurant offers a six-course prix-fixe menu, newly created each evening. Its celebrated wine cellar boasts over a thousand selections, earning *Wine Spectator's* prestigious "Best of Award of Excellence."

Visit Antrim 1844 today and rediscover the genteel spirit of 19th-century America, when grace and elegance were the bastion of great hotels.

GRILLED LAMB FILLET
WITH APPLE ALMOND COMPOTE

Serves 6

1¹⁄₂ pounds sugar

2 pounds apples, cored and sliced

10 ounces almonds

7 ounces vinegar

Pinch rosemary

4 pounds lamb fillets

9 ounces butter, cubed

In a sauté pan, cook the sugar over low heat until golden brown and caramelized. Add apples and almonds. Cook for 1 minute. Add vinegar and cook 1 minute longer. Add rosemary.

Grill lamb fillets. Stir butter into the compote. Serve the lamb sliced or whole on a bed of apple almond compote.

MELON SOUP

Serves 6

1 cantaloupe
1 honeydew
4 tablespoons white wine, *divided*
$1/8$ teaspoon vanilla extract
Pinch salt
2 tablespoons Midori
Fresh mint leaves
Whipped cream

Carefully remove the rind from both melons; slice in half and remove seeds. Cut fruit into chunks; set honeydew aside. In a blender or food processor, purée the cantaloupe with 2 tablespoons wine, vanilla and salt.

In another blender, purée the honeydew with Midori, a few mint leaves and remaining wine. Refrigerate both soups until chilled.

To serve, pour each soup at the same time into either side of a bowl. Garnish with whipped cream and more mint leaves.

Note: Using a blender will result in a smoother soup. For best results, serve in clear glass bowls or martini glasses.

TAPENADE

Serves 6

4 ounces black olives
2 ounces green olives
$1 1/4$ ounces anchovies
2 ounces olive oil
$1 1/2$ teaspoons mustard
1 teaspoon Cognac

Place all ingredients in a food processor; purée just until coarsely chopped.

GAZPACHO

Serves 12

2 pounds ripe tomatoes
2 large cucumbers
$1/2$ large green bell pepper
1 clove garlic
1 shallot
$1/2$ tablespoon chopped parsley
$1/2$ tablespoon chopped basil
1 tablespoon white wine vinegar

Juice of 1 lime
4 dashes Tabasco
Salt and pepper to taste

Cut the tomatoes, cucumbers and green pepper into pieces; place in a food processor or blender. Add remaining ingredients; process until combined. Chill before serving.

The Greenbrier

If the walls of this resort could talk, oh, the stories they could tell. From its beginnings as a place of "healing waters" ... to serving as a Civil War headquarters, WWII hospital and 1950s bomb shelter ... to hosting golf's prestigious Ryder Cup ... the Greenbrier has a long and fascinating history.

For its first 125 years, the resort was known as White Sulphur Springs due to the spring of sulphur water at the center of the property. It's located below the green dome of the white-columned Springhouse, which has been the symbol of the Greenbrier for generations. Starting in 1778, people came to "take the waters" to restore their health.

Development proceeded slowly until a stagecoach route was carved through the forested mountains of West Virginia. By the 1830s, the resort attained its first period of prominence as planters, judges, lawyers and merchants from Southern states began to congregate in the village in summer.

The resort originally consisted of rows of cottages, many of which still stand today, including Paradise Row, Alabama Row and Baltimore Row. The cottages of Baltimore Row were designed by John H.B. Latrobe, a Baltimore lawyer who was the son of famed architect Benjamin Latrobe. His style extended to the later Tansas, South Carolina and Florida Rows and became the basis for the design of the new Copeland Hill cottages.

By the eve of the Civil War, White Sulphur Springs' reputation as the most fashionable social resort in the Southern states was well-established, and this led to the addition in 1858 of the first large hotel on the property, officially named the Grand Central Hotel, but known to longtime patrons as the Old White Hotel.

During the war, the resort was closed. Over the course of the conflict, both sides occupied the grounds, using the hotel either as a hospital or military headquarters. Shortly after the war's end, the resort reopened and its prospects were enhanced with the arrival of the Chesapeake and Ohio Railway. For the next 100 years, White Sulphur Springs was one of the classic railroad resorts in the country. Trains brought visitors from New York, Washington, Richmond, Atlanta, Louisville, Chicago, Cleveland and scores of points in between.

In 1910, the Chesapeake and Ohio Railway purchased the property and embarked upon a major expansion. By 1913, the railroad had added the Greenbrier Hotel (the central portion of today's hotel), a new Mineral Bath Department (the building that includes the pool) and an 18-hole golf course (now called the Old White Course) designed by the most prominent golf architect of the day, Charles Blair Macdonald.

The resort was open year-round for the first time in 1914, the year President and Mrs. Woodrow Wilson spent their Easter holiday at the Greenbrier, and Joseph and Rose Kennedy traveled down from Boston for their October honeymoon Business was booming in the '20s as the Greenbrier took its place on the fashionable society resort circuit that stretched from Palm Beach,

The Greenbrier

300 West Main Street

White Sulphur Springs,

   West Virginia 24986

(304) 536-1110

(800) 453-4858

www.greenbrier.com

Florida, to Newport, Rhode Island.

The Old White Hotel, designed for summer use only, was torn down in 1922. That led to a substantial expansion and rebuilding of the Greenbrier Hotel at the end of the decade. Along with redesigning the main entrance, Cleveland architect Philip Small added the Virginia Wing to the south and added what is now the signature north entrance façade. He mixed elements from the resort's Southern historical roots with motifs from the Old White Hotel.

During World War II, the Greenbrier was put to two quite different uses by the U.S. Government. The State Department leased the hotel for seven months after the U.S. entry into the war and used it to intern German, Japanese and Italian diplomatic personnel until they could be exchanged for American diplomats stranded overseas.

In September 1942, the U.S. Army purchased the Greenbrier, converted it into a 2,000-bed hospital and renamed it Ashford General Hospital. For four years, the resort served as a surgical and rehabilitation center, where 24,148 soldiers were treated.

The Chesapeake and Ohio Railway reacquired the property in 1946 and initiated a comprehensive redecoration of the hotel interior by noted decorator Dorothy Draper (whose résumé also includes the Fairmont San Francisco). The origin of the Greenbrier's distinctive décor goes back to Draper's legendary postwar redecoration, when she was at the peak of her fame. Carleton Varney took over her firm when she retired in the 1960s, and he has decorated the Greenbrier for over three decades.

When the Greenbrier reopened in 1948, Sam Snead returned to where his career had begun in 1936. For many years, he was the Golf Pro Emeritus, until his death in May 2002. More than any other individual, he established the Greenbrier's reputation as one of the foremost golf resorts in the world.

In the late 1950s, the Federal Government once again approached the Greenbrier for assistance, this time in the construction of an Emergency Relocation Center for the use of Congress in case of war. The classified, underground bomb shelter was built in conjunction with the addition of the West Virginia Wing to the hotel. For 30 years, the owners maintained an agreement with the government that in the case of an international crisis, the entire property would be conveyed to government use.

Aboveground, life proceeded normally, as the historic cottages were upgraded ... extensive conference facilities added ... and the Greenbrier Course rebuilt, under the direction of Jack Nicklaus—in short, all the things necessary to stay competitive in an increasingly crowded luxury resort market of the 1980s and '90s. The Greenbrier was also the venue for two international golf matches, the Ryder Cup and Solheim Cup.

Because of the agreement with the government, most of the property was not available for residential development until the underground shelter was closed down in 1995.

You have several convenient options to travel to the Greenbrier—fly, drive or, like some of the early visitors, take a train. However you arrive, be prepared for a luxurious stay in a magnificent place brimming with history.

TAVERN FIVE-ONION SOUP

This is a longtime favorite in the Greenbrier's Tavern Room. The key is cooking the onions very slowly until they are well caramelized. You can prepare the soup in advance through the puréeing step, then reheat and add the cream just before serving. The crispy shallots may be made ahead, too.

Serves 8–10

2 tablespoons butter

3 medium shallots, sliced

1 small leek (white portion only), trimmed and sliced

1 small red onion, sliced

1 medium yellow onion, sliced

6 green onions (white portion) only, sliced

1/4 cup white wine

1 tablespoon sugar

6 cups strong chicken stock

Bouquet garni (2 sprigs thyme, 2 parsley stems, 4 peppercorns and 1 bay leaf)

1 cup heavy whipping cream

Salt and pepper to taste

Crispy Fried Shallots

Canola oil for frying

2 shallots, halved lengthwise and thinly sliced

1 tablespoon all-purpose flour

Melt butter in a large heavy saucepan. Add the shallots, leek and all of the onions. Cook over medium heat, stirring occasionally, until onions are soft, 10–12 minutes. Deglaze the pan with wine and cook until evaporated. Sprinkle with sugar and stir to incorporate.

Press a piece of aluminum foil onto the surface of the onions and continue cooking. Stir from time to time, scraping the bottom of the pot to ensure the onions are not sticking or burning. Cook until onions are meltingly soft or a deep golden brown.

Remove foil. Add stock and bouquet garni; simmer, uncovered, for 20 minutes. Remove from the heat. Discard bouquet garni. Purée the soup in batches in a food processor. Place soup in a clean pan; add cream and bring to a simmer. Simmer for a few minutes to reduce slightly if needed. Season with salt and pepper.

For fried shallots, add about 2 inches of oil to a small heavy pot. Heat over medium-high heat. Coat shallots with flour; shake in a strainer to remove excess flour. Drop the shallots, a few at a time, into hot oil and stir to keep from sticking together. Cook slowly to a deep golden brown. Remove with a slotted spoon and drain in a single layer on paper towels. (Shallots may be fried up to 8 hours ahead and stored in an airtight container.)

To serve, ladle soup into warm bowls. Sprinkle with crispy fried shallots. Garnish with chopped chives if desired.

The Grove Park Inn Resort & Spa

The Grove Park Inn Resort
    & Spa

290 Macon Avenue

Asheville, North Carolina

    28804

(828) 252-2711

(800) 438-5800

www.groveparkinn.com

A hotel "built not for the present alone, but for ages to come, and the admiration of generations yet unborn." This was the dream of Edwin Wiley Grove (1850–1927) of Tennessee, owner of a pharmaceutical firm in St. Louis that produced Grove's Bromo-Quinine and Grove's Tasteless Chill Tonic. Suffering from bronchitis, he came to Asheville as a summer resident and found the climate to be so beneficial to his health that he bought land here, including a large acreage on Sunset Mountain.

Planning to build a unique resort overlooking the mountains he had come to love, he consulted many architects, but none could grasp his idea. So he turned to Fred Seeley, his son-in-law. Without an architect or a contractor, this remarkable man built a remarkable edifice.

Granite stones (some of them weighing as much as 10,000 pounds) were taken from Sunset Mountain, hauled to the site by wagon trains and fitted into place by Italian stonemasons and hundreds of local laborers. Built in 11 months and 27 days, the hotel opened on July 12, 1913, with William Jennings Bryan delivering the official address.

Known as the "Big Room," the lobby was 120 feet long and 80 feet wide, with elevators running through the chimney rock work, and massive fireplaces large enough to burn 112-foot logs. A superb orchestral organ, with 7,000 pipes, was built for the hotel by Ernest Skinner of Boston. It was sold in 1927 for $75,000.

Grove leased his hotel from 1914 to 1927 to Seeley, who was his manager. His policies, though appreciated by his conservative clientele at the time, would seem a bit austere now: children were discouraged, pets forbidden; only low tones and whispers were permitted after 10:30 p.m.; and slamming of doors was not allowed. As the inn literature stated, this was necessary "to maintain a place where tired, busy people can get away from all annoyances and rest their nerves."

Many famous names appeared on the early guest registers, including Thomas Edison, Harvey Firestone, Henry Ford, Woodrow Wilson, the Roosevelts, General Dwight Eisenhower and F. Scott Fitzgerald, who spent the summer of 1936 at the hotel while his wife, Zelda, was in Asheville's Highland Hospital.

During World War II, the U.S. Government leased the inn, and Axis diplomats were interned here in 1942 while awaiting repatriation. Though completely cut off from the outside world, they were treated as ordinary guests, paying their own expenses. At the end of 1942, the Navy Department converted the inn to a rest center for Navy personnel. From 1944 until the end of the war, the hotel was part of an Army Redistribution Station, where soldiers back from overseas duty rested before being reassigned.

The property changed hands many times until 1955, when it was purchased by Dallas entrepreneur Charles A. Sammons.

The Fairway Lodge and North Wing were added in 1958 and 1964 (since removed), and in 1976, the adjoining Country Club of Asheville—with its 18-hole golf course, pool and clubhouse—was purchased. The inn was named to the National Register of Historic Places in 1973.

A new era began in 1982, when a multimillion-dollar expansion program was launched. The Main Inn was renovated, the Sammons Wing added and the Country Club remodeled. In 1984, the once-seasonal resort opened year-round. Further expansion has included an Indoor Sports Complex, the luxurious 10-story Vanderbilt Wing and a 40,000-square-foot spa.

Because of the vision and efforts of Charles Sammons (1898–1988) and his wife, Elaine, who is currently chairman of the board, Dr. Grove's dream had become a reality. Now restored and expanded, the Grove Park Inn Resort has entered the 21st century and will surely garner the "admiration of generations yet unborn."

STONE-GROUND GRITS AND SHRIMP

Serves 4

2 cups whole milk

2 cups water

1 cup stone-ground grits

1 teaspoon salt

6 tablespoons unsalted butter, cubed, *divided*

1 cup heavy whipping cream

2 teaspoons freshly ground pepper

2 tablespoons vegetable oil

1¹/₂ pounds (21-25 count) shrimp, peeled and deveined

3 shallots, chopped

1 clove garlic, chopped

1 cup strong brewed coffee

¹/₄ teaspoon dried thyme

¹/₂ teaspoon brown sugar

Additional salt and freshly ground pepper

In a heavy saucepan over medium heat, bring milk and water to a boil. Add grits and salt. Reduce heat to low; simmer for 30 minutes, stirring occasionally. Add 4 tablespoons butter, cream and pepper; simmer 5 minutes longer. Serve immediately or keep warm in a double boiler.

Heat oil in a large skillet until hot. Sauté shrimp and shallots for 3 minutes. Add garlic; sauté 1 minute longer. Add coffee, thyme and brown sugar. Bring to a boil. Season to taste with salt and pepper. Remove from the heat; fold in remaining butter. Serve over grits.

WILD MUSHROOM RISOTTO

Serves 6-8

³/₄ cup butter, *divided*

1 cup diced yellow onion

1¹/₂ cups uncooked risotto

1 teaspoon cracked black pepper

¹/₂ cup white wine

2 cups chicken broth, *divided*

1 cup half-and-half cream, *divided*

2 cups julienned mushrooms

1¹/₂ cups grated Parmesan cheese

1 clove garlic, minced

1 tablespoon chopped fresh thyme

¹/₂ cup chopped scallions

¹/₂ cup green peas

¹/₂ cup diced carrots

In a saucepan over medium-high heat, melt ¼ cup butter. Add onion, risotto and pepper. Cook and stir for 3–4 minutes to activate the starch (be sure to not brown the grains). Cover with wine and 1 cup broth. Bring to a slow boil. When the mixture gets close to absorbing the liquid, continue to add some butter, broth and cream.

Just before risotto is done, add mushrooms, Parmesan cheese and the rest of the butter. Add the garlic, thyme, scallions, peas and carrots last, along with enough cream to finish the cooking process.

CRANBERRY-PUMPKIN BREAD PUDDING

Serves 6–8

4 to 6 cups bread cubes
   (biscuits or croissants are best)
1 cup fresh cranberries
8 eggs
4 cups milk
1 can (15 ounces) solid-pack pumpkin
½ tablespoon vanilla extract
1 cup sugar
1 tablespoon ground cinnamon
1 teaspoon ground cloves
1 teaspoon ground nutmeg

Place bread cubes in a 13-inch x 9-inch x 2-inch baking dish, using enough to fill the dish. Sprinkle with cranberries. Blend the remaining ingredients; pour over berries and bread, making sure all the cubes are submerged (push down if necessary). Bake at 350° for 1 hour or until set.

The Homestead

The Homestead

1766 Homestead Drive

Hot Springs, Virginia 24445

(540) 839-1766

(866) 354-4653

www.thehomestead.com

Ten years before the American Revolution, the Homestead was already a place apart from the tensions and stress of everyday life. For over two centuries, the resort has provided an oasis of relaxation at its magnificent location in the Allegheny Mountains of Virginia.

Colonial explorers began to visit the area in the 1720s. Like the Native Americans before them, they traveled along buffalo trails and discovered the natural mineral springs that have always been an integral part of the fabric of the region. By 1750, homesteaders had constructed simple wooden guest cabins near the most desirable springs, attracting travelers from across the eastern seaboard. They wrote about what was believed to be the medicinal properties of the springs, as well as the scenic beauty and gentle climate.

George Washington, 23 years old and commanding the Virginia Militia, visited these springs in 1755 and 1756 and became friends with Thomas Bullett, who had begun to survey the region and who also served as an officer in the Militia. Officers were paid for their service in land, and on June 27, 1764, Bullett and his partners received a grant of 300 acres, which included seven mineral springs.

Bullett took the lead in developing the area, convincing Militia members under his command to homestead there. Under his direction, the spring pools were improved, a rustic wooden lodge was completed in 1766 and the Homestead was born.

In 1832, the Homestead was acquired by Dr. Thomas Goode, who is credited with some of its greatest innovations and growth. A prominent Virginia physician, he visited renowned spas in Europe and brought back from his travels a revolutionary hydrotherapy treatment: the Spout Bath. This treatment, renowned for its ability to simultaneously relieve tension and promote tranquillity, is still offered today.

Just as Capt. Bullett was the first to recognize the potential of the springs as a spa resort, Dr. Goode was the first to recognize its potential for fine dining. His addition of spacious dining rooms, new kitchens and a beautiful ballroom set the stage. The resort is well-known as a destination for exceptional cuisine, and dancing continues to be a nightly tradition and a central part of the dining experience.

After Goode's death in 1858, the Homestead had a succession of owners. Then, in 1888, financier J. Pierpont Morgan and a number of other wealthy investors purchased the facility, recognizing its great potential. Morgan's name in association with any venture was certain to attract investors, and many of his banking partners and business associates also bought into the enterprise.

By 1892, a massive and sustained building campaign was well under way. The results were astonishing, and the "Grande Dame of the Mountains" took on a new and exciting luster. All of the old buildings were razed, a new main Homestead hotel was built and an imposing new wing was added. Guestrooms and suites were elegantly furnished; Thomas Edison (a regular guest) supplied the first electric power plant; and the latest recreational activities were installed.

Perhaps the most exciting project was construction of the new Spa (originally called the Bath House) in 1892. After extensive research, the most advanced European spa services and the latest in physical fitness were added to the traditional treatments.

At the dawn of the 20th century, relaxation began to mean recreation for more American families. Equestrian activities were enhanced with a new stable. The Homestead was first among Southern resorts to offer golf, badminton, tennis and ten-pin bowling.

Golf also came to the Homestead in 1892 with construction of the first six holes of the Old Course. The first tee of the Old Course enjoys the distinction of being the oldest first tee in continuous use in America. The game quickly became so popular that the Old Course was expanded to 18 holes, and later a second course was built. The Cascades Course has enjoyed an outstanding history, hosting seven USGA championships and two Senior PGA Tour Shoot-Outs. Robert Trent Jones designed a third course, the Lower Cascades.

The first of the buildings seen and enjoyed today opened for guests in March 1902. These new buildings were fashioned of red brick, limestone and steel, in the most elegant and classical style of architecture. Conveniences then rarely seen in the homes of the wealthiest Americans were now commonplace at the Homestead, where every room had electricity, steam heat, an indoor bathroom with a tub plus hot and cold running water, and a wall-mounted, crank-type telephone.

Steady patronage precipitated many additions. The West Wing was opened in 1904 and immediately became the favorite of the Vanderbilt clan. The East Wing was completed in 1914, and the Theatre, Crystal Room, Empire Room and Garden Room debuted in 1923. By the late '20s, additional space was again required, and the Tower was opened in 1929. Situated on that original 300-acre land grant, the Tower remains the hallmark of the resort.

J.P. Morgan took a personal interest in the Homestead, arriving in his private railroad car for visits. In fact, he retained his majority investment throughout his life.

During World War II, the Homestead hosted Japanese diplomats and their families for a short time, and it was the site of the United Nations Conference on Food and Agriculture in 1943. The Homestead became the pioneer Southern ski resort, when the first slopes were added in 1959.

As the last decade of the 20th century dawned, the Homestead had seen better days. Fortunately, new owners gave the resort a new lease on life to delight visitors well into the 21st century.

Entering the Presidents Lounge for cocktails, you are surrounded by the portraits of the 22 Presidents who have all visited the Homestead, together with the portrait of George Washington, whose travels in the area predate the resort itself. A visit to this National Historic Landmark is truly a trip into the past.

The Homestead

HUMMUS

Makes about 1 cup

1 cup canned chickpeas (garbanzo beans)
1 clove garlic, peeled
1/3 cup sesame oil
1/2 cup lemon juice
1/4 teaspoon salt
3 teaspoons chopped fresh parsley, *divided*

Drain the chickpeas in a fine mesh sieve. Press the garlic clove through a garlic press into a blender; add the oil, lemon juice and salt. Blend on medium speed for a few seconds. Add the chickpeas and 2 teaspoons parsley; purée on high speed until creamy and smooth. Chill for at least 1 hour before serving. Spoon into a serving bowl; sprinkle with remaining parsley.

Known in Arabic as "hummus bi tahina" (tahina is sesame seed paste), this delicious paste is a staple food in the Middle East. There, it is either eaten as is, scooped up with little pieces of pita bread or used as a dip for raw vegetables.

MOUSSE Á LA FRAMBOISE

Serves 16

4 cups fresh raspberries
1/3 cup sugar
Juice of 1/2 lemon
3 tablespoons framboise (raspberry liqueur)
4 teaspoons unflavored gelatin
1/4 cup cold water
2 cups heavy whipping cream

Purée the raspberries in a blender or food processor; force the purée through a fine mesh sieve. Discard seeds. With a rubber spatula, transfer the purée to a 2-quart bowl (4 cups raspberries should yield about 2 cups purée). Whisk in the sugar, lemon juice and framboise. Taste and adjust the flavor if necessary, depending upon the sweetness of the berries. Set aside.

In a small bowl, sprinkle gelatin over cold water; let stand until softened. Pour the cream into a 1-quart bowl; whip with a hand mixer until stiff. In a small saucepan, heat softened gelatin until dissolved. Stir into the raspberry mixture. Fold in whipped cream. Pour into a 2-quart soufflé dish. Chill for at least 4 hours before serving.

When the hot, humid days of summer produce a bumper crop of red raspberries, make a purée, mix it with whipped cream and chill ... you will please even the most fastidious berry devotee.

"There is no love sincerer than the love of food."
–George Bernard Shaw

The Hotel Hershey

The Hotel Hershey

100 Hotel Road

Hershey, Pennyslvania 17033

(717) 533-2171

(800) 437-7439

www.thehotelhershey.com

While the nation was suffering through the Great Depression, the "Chocolate King," Milton S. Hershey, had a vision. Though close friends and associates called him crazy and urged him not to do it, he was determined to build a grand hotel high atop Pat's Hill in the town he built on chocolate.

Nearly three decades earlier, Hershey had perfected his formula for milk chocolate and began his planned community of Hershey, Pennsylvania. He had already constructed the chocolate factory, homes for his employees and a school for orphaned boys. Now it was time to realize his dream.

Before his wife, Catherine, passed away in 1915, she and Milton had planned to build a luxury hotel in the style of those they loved during their travels abroad. They dreamed of re-creating the Heliopolis Hotel, a famous resort in Cairo, Egypt. Hershey went so far as to purchase the architectural plans, but when the estimated cost to duplicate the structure was $5 million, he abandoned the idea.

In 1930, Hershey announced that he intended to build his hotel after all. He gave his architect, D. Paul Witmer, a postcard of a smaller hotel he and Catherine had enjoyed on the Mediterranean. His involvement didn't stop there. Based on travel notes he and his wife had kept, Hershey instructed Witmer to outfit the new hotel with a Spanish patio, tiled floors, a fountain, and a dining room with a good view from every table.

During construction, as many as 800 steelworkers, masons, carpenters, and other craftsmen and laborers were employed on the Hershey payroll. "We have about 600 construction workers in this town," Hershey said. "If I don't provide work for them, I'll have to feed them. And since building materials are now at their lowest cost levels, I'm going to build and give them jobs."

Work began in 1932, continued through a very mild winter and was completed in 1933. A formal opening celebration was held on May 26, 1933 with a dinner and dance for 400 invited guests. The $2 million Hotel Hershey opened for business the next day. It was an elegant jewel nestled in the rolling hills of Hershey's birthplace.

A local newspaper observed, "Somewhat belying the simplicity of taste for which the 'Chocolate King' is noted, the hotel is characterized by great luxury of detail and elegance of appointment. Tinted walls, palms and fountains, carved woodwork, and brilliant hangings and rugs."

Indeed, a Mediterranean-style hotel in central Pennsylvania was unarguably distinctive. Among its unique features, the Circular Dining Room promised what Hershey wanted—a view from every table. Built in a semicircle, without pillars or corners, it allows each guest to view the breathtaking formal gardens on the far side of the windows. Thirteen stained glass windows frame the outside perimeter, with each pane depicting birds and blooms native to Hershey's beloved state.

The Hotel Hershey celebrates over 70 years of tradition and elegance.

HERSHEY'S CHOCOLATE CREAM PIE

2 ¹/₂ cups milk, *divided*

1 cup sugar

3 tablespoons all-purpose flour

5 tablespoons cornstarch

¹/₂ teaspoon salt

3 egg yolks

2 ¹/₂ ounces unsweetened baking chocolate

2 tablespoons butter

1 ¹/₂ teaspoons vanilla extract

1 pastry shell (9 inches), baked

In a 1-quart saucepan, heat 1½ cups milk and sugar. In a mixing bowl, combine the flour, cornstarch and salt. Add egg yolks and remaining milk; mix well. Temper this mixture by adding a third of the hot milk mixture. Return all to the saucepan. Bring to a boil; boil and stir for 1 minute.

Remove from the heat. Add chocolate and stir until melted. Finish with butter and vanilla. Pour into pastry shell. Refrigerate until set.

"NUTRAGEOUS" CHOCOLATE CAKE

Serves 10
Chocolate Flourless Sponge Cake

3 ¼ cups egg whites

1 ¼ cups sugar

3 cups egg yolks

¾ cup cocoa powder

Chocolate Mousse

5 ¼ teaspoons unflavored gelatin

5 tablespoons cold water

2 ¾ cups milk

2 ¼ cups egg yolks

1 cup sugar

2 milk chocolate couvertures (3 ounces *each*)*

12 ounces hazelnut paste

2 ¼ quarts heavy whipping cream

Peanut Glaze

2 ¼ quarts chocolate ganache

14 ounces peanuts, toasted and chopped

In a mixing bowl, beat egg whites and sugar until very stiff. Fold in egg yolks and add cocoa powder. Pour into two greased 10-inch round cake pans. Bake at 400° for 10–15 minutes. Cool for 10 minutes; remove cakes from pans to wire racks.

For the mousse, in a small bowl, soften gelatin in cold water; set aside. In a saucepan, bring milk to a boil. Beat the egg yolks and sugar; temper with some of the hot milk, then pour the entire mixture into the saucepan. Whisk in softened gelatin until completely dissolved. Place chocolate and hazelnut paste in a bowl; pour hot mixture over the top.

Transfer to a mixing bowl. With the whisk attachment, beat until cold and fluffy. Whip cream to a soft peak; fold into mousse. Immediately pipe onto one cake round. Top with second cake round.

Combine ganache and peanuts; pour over filled cake. Don't wait too long to move it off the rack as the glaze will become hard. Slice cake and serve with caramel ice cream.

Couverture is professional-quality coating chocolate found in specialty and candy-making shops.

"*I never eat when I can dine.*"

—Maurice Chevalier

Hotel Monaco

Housed in what was once Washington, D.C.'s General Post Office, Hotel Monaco is a National Historic Landmark that has reflected the grandeur of the U.S. capital for more than 150 years. Occupying an entire block in the heart of the vibrant downtown arts and theater district, the 184-room boutique hotel is easily accessible to all the city has to offer.

Throughout the 18th and 19th centuries, this area was the "center city" of Washington. In 1795, the first known structure to occupy this site was Blodgett's Hotel, which was built to promote real estate development plans for the city of Washington. Congress purchased the site in 1810 for the General Post Office, which occupied the first floor, and the Patent Office, which occupied the upper floors.

Dr. William Thornton saved the building from destruction in 1812, when Admiral George Cockburn ordered British troops to burn all public property in the city. After the fire, it was the only building available large enough to house Congress. On September 19, 1814, the third session of the 13th Congress convened there. The building did not survive another blaze—it was destroyed by an accidental fire in 1836.

The southern part of the current structure was designed by Robert Mills, architect of the Washington Monument. Completed in 1842, it was the first all-marble building in the city and was again occupied by the General Post Office. Regarded as avant-garde for the time, Mills

patterned the building after the first marble building in Rome, the Temple of Jupiter.

Over a decade later, Thomas Walter, one of the architects of the United States Capitol, created the design for an extension on the north side of the building, which was completed in 1869. The building later housed the Tariff Commission and became known as the Tariff Building.

Recently, the building was completely rehabilitated into the 184-room Hotel Monaco. Architects worked tirelessly to ensure that the historical significance and architectural grandeur of the building were maintained.

The hotel's exterior is graced with the original Roman Corinthian columns of rich white marble. Inside, there's an element of surprise—designers juxtaposed the classical 19th-century architecture with modern 20th-century furnishings. In a playful nod, a bust of the third President, Thomas Jefferson, overlooks each guestroom.

When it opened, *Condé Nast Traveler* named Hotel Monaco one of "80 Best New Hotels in the world," and in 2005 featured the hotel on its "2005 Gold List" as one of "The World's Best Places to Stay."

Offering all the comforts of home (assuming you have 15-foot vaulted ceilings, that is), Hotel Monaco even allows guests to bring along their pets. For those who choose to leave their pets behind, companion goldfish are part of the temporary pet program. Another unique offering is the 20 specially designed "Tall

Hotel Monaco

700 F Street NW

Washington, D.C. 20002

(202) 628-7177

(800) 649-1202

www.hotelmonaco-dc.com

Rooms"—20 guestrooms customized for tall people, featuring extra-long beds (90 inches), high ceilings and raised showerheads.

Adjacent to the hotel in the historic courtyard, the Poste Moderne Brasserie is a 174-seat restaurant and bar that appeals to locals, visitors and groups looking for a unique dining experience. The restaurant's main entrance is accessed through the historic carriageway portal on 8th Street. The upscale contemporary brasserie, with a striking exhibition kitchen, offers modern American cuisine and a wine list featuring American, European and Australian wines. Outdoor seating is available in warm weather.

With a close proximity to the MCI Center, Shakespeare Theater, National Portrait Gallery, Washington Convention Center and the new Spy Museum, Hotel Monaco serves business travelers, tourists and residents looking for a great meal.

HAMACHI, RUBY RED GRAPEFRUIT AND GINGER VINAIGRETTE

Serves 8

2 drops orange oil

2 drops Banyuls vinegar

$1/2$ teaspoon finely grated ginger

2 teaspoons soy sauce

$1/2$ teaspoon finely crushed garlic

1 cup grapeseed oil

Salt and pepper to taste

Sliced ginger

8 ounces Hamachi (kingfish), thinly sliced

2 ruby red grapefruit, segmented

2 blood oranges, segmented

For garnish—baby cilantro, thinly sliced scallions,
   finely julienned parsley, micro spinach,
   chopped chives and chive sprigs

For the vinaigrette, combine the orange oil, vinegar, grated ginger, soy sauce and garlic; slowly add grapeseed oil. Season with salt and pepper.

For crispy ginger, blanch and shock young ginger slices; crisp slowly in grapeseed oil.

To serve, arrange Hamachi and citrus on plates. Drizzle with vinaigrette. Garnish with crispy ginger, greens and herbs.

"The qualities of an exceptional cook are akin to those of a successful tightrope walker: an abiding passion for the task, courage to go out on a limb and an impeccable sense of balance."

—Bryan Miller

Park Hyatt Philadelphia at the Bellevue

Park Hyatt Philadelphia at
the Bellevue
Broad & Walnut Streets
Philadelphia, Pennsylvania
19102
(215) 893-1234
www.parkphiladephia.hyatt.
com

Known worldwide as Philadelphia's preeminent hotel, the Bellevue is referred to as "The Grande Dame of Broad Street." Since 1904, when it was opened by Waldorf=Astoria manager George C. Boldt as the Bellevue-Stratford, the hotel has been frequented by royalty, celebrities, socialites, luminaries and heads of state.

The hotel, which took two years to build, was erected in French Renaissance style architecture. It features Gilded Age architectural flourishes, including the most magnificent two-tiered ballroom in the United States, with delicate lighting fixtures designed by Thomas Edison, stained glass by Louis Comfort Tiffany, and the most celebrated circular staircases in the city.

Every U.S. President since Theodore Roosevelt has visited the Bellevue. Other notable guests include Jacob Astor, J.P. Morgan, William Jennings Bryan, Bob Hope, Jimmy Durante, John Wayne, Katharine Hepburn and the Vanderbilt family.

For a century, the hotel has been regarded historically as the location for several of America's premier society galas, including the Academy Ball, the Charity Ball and the Assemblies. It was the site of the 1948 Democratic National Convention, and the 1936 and 1948 Republican National Conventions. The Bellevue was also headquarters for the U.S. Navy each year during the Army-Navy game and hosted the pregame dinner gala.

In June of 1978, Richard I. Rubin Associates purchased the former Bellevue-Stratford, paying $8,250,000—a sum nearly equivalent to the original cost of construction in 1904. They saw great potential in saving the landmark building from demolition and renovating the property, in support of the revitalization of Broad Street, Philadelphia's premier arts and cultural destination, now referred to as the "Avenue of the Arts."

In December 1996, Hyatt Hotels Corporation assumed management of the hotel facility, occupying the top seven floors of the Bellevue, and renamed it the Park Hyatt Philadelphia at the Bellevue.

The Bellevue is also the place for fine dining at the critically acclaimed Palm Restaurant and the equally renowned Zanzibar Blue jazz club as well as the domed splendor of the Founders Restaurant.

STARS AND STRIPES CRAB SOUP

Serves 10

2 quarts low-sodium chicken *or* vegetable stock
2 teaspoons salt
8 ounces star-shaped pastina
1 can (6 ounces) tomato paste
1 can (16 ounces) tomato purée
1 tablespoon minced garlic
1 tablespoon dried basil
1 can claw crabmeat
1$^1/_4$ cups chopped fresh parsley

In a soup pot, bring stock to a boil. Add salt and pasta. When pasta is tender, whisk in tomato paste. Then add tomato purée, garlic and basil. Break up crab and add to the pot; stir in gently. Garnish with parsley.

CONSTITUTION CANAPÉ
A RED, WHITE & BLUE PLATE LOBSTER SPECIAL

1 small bunch fresh chives

¹/₄ cup extra virgin olive oil

1 East Coast lobster (2 pounds), steamed, shelled and separated by knuckle, claw and tail

¹/₄ cup heavy whipping cream

Sea salt and ground white pepper to taste

2 tablespoons butter

Juice and zest of ¹/₂ medium lemon

1 tablespoon red tobikko caviar (available at specialty food stores)

3 Peruvian blue potatoes

4 slices brioche, toasted and lightly brushed with butter

Fresh chervil sprigs

For chive oil, blanch the chives in a boiling-water bath lightly seasoned with salt; shock in an ice-water bath. Pat completely dry. In a food processor fitted with a steel blade, purée the chives. Add oil and pulse for 10 seconds. Pass mixture through several layers of cheesecloth; allow to rest in a small ceramic bowl. Once the oil has settled, transfer to a squeeze bottle and reserve.

Reserve the red lobster meat. For the lobster mousse, purée the white tail meat, using a food processor fitted with a steel blade. Slowly add heavy cream while the blade is in motion. Season with salt and pepper. When the lobster is fluffy, add butter and whip until incorporated. Set aside.

Mince the lobster meat from the claw and knuckle and the reserved meat from the tail. Season with lemon zest, salt and pepper. Drizzle with lemon juice. Add the caviar and incorporate. Hold at room temperature.

Boil the potatoes until tender; purée and season, then finish with butter.

Cut the brioche with 2-inch star-shaped cutters; brush both sides with olive oil. Place on a silpat-lined baking sheet. Bake at 350° for 2 minutes or until lightly colored.

To assemble, place a 1-inch biscuit cutter (with 1¼-inch cylinder walls) in the center of brioche star. Using a pastry bag fitted with a medium plain tip, pipe potato purée in the lower third of the cutter. Follow with lobster mousse in a pastry bag with a star tip. Follow next with the caviar-lobster mixture. Place a small star of lobster mousse on top. Garnish with a sprig of chervil; drizzle serving plate with chive oil.

PHILADELPHIA FREEDOM
LOBSTER PEPPERPOT SOUP

Serves 4

2 Idaho potatoes

2 carrots

3 celery ribs

2 large portobello mushroom caps

1 large yellow onion

1 red bell pepper

1 green bell pepper

1 quart water

2½ pounds Maine lobster

2 tablespoons butter

1 sprig fresh thyme

½ tablespoon kosher salt

8 turns black pepper

1 cup white wine

2 bay leaves

3 cloves garlic, smashed

3 tablespoons olive oil

2 cups smashed peeled plum tomatoes

4 slices cornbread, toasted and buttered

Peel potatoes and carrots; dice into 1-inch pieces. Dice celery, mushrooms, onion and peppers into 1-inch pieces; set aside.

Bring water to a boil; steam lobster for 12 minutes. Reserve water. Remove claws and tail. Rinse and chop head and body. In a skillet, sauté lobster meat in butter until body turns red. Add thyme, salt, pepper and wine. Bring to a hard simmer for 12 minutes.

In a soup pot, sauté potatoes, carrots, celery, mushrooms, onion, peppers, bay leaves and garlic in oil until they begin to take color. Strain in lobster stock; add tomatoes. Simmer for 15 minutes. Remove claw and tail meat from lobster; chop and add to soup. Serve piping hot with toasted cornbread.

"The best number for a dinner party is two: myself and a darn good headwaiter."

–Nubar Gulbenkian

Williamsburg Inn

Conceived and built by John D. Rockefeller Jr. and opened in April 1937, the Williamsburg Inn remains today the crown jewel of the five Colonial Williamsburg Hotels. The inn was built in just one year, necessitated by the early, immediate success of the adjacent Historic Area, which is today a 301-acre living interpretation of colonial Virginia's history.

The Colonial Williamsburg Foundation restored the town to its 18th-century splendor beginning in 1926 under the direction of Williamsburg rector and historian Dr. W.A.R. Goodwin. Rockefeller was so inspired by Goodwin's passion for the project that he became a partner.

Because so many visitors to Colonial Williamsburg were personal friends of Rockefeller and his wife, Abby Aldrich, the couple became involved in every aspect of the inn's design, construction and furnishings. They felt strongly that it should be as unlike a traditional hotel as possible, preferring the furnishings and décor to have the ambience of a gracious country residence.

Working with renowned Boston architect William Perry, they designed and decorated the inn in the Regency style of early 19th-century England. The couple traveled throughout Europe in search of furnishings and even had a "sample" guestroom built so they could visualize the décor.

The architectural style was specifically chosen in contrast to the Colonial architecture of the neighboring Historic Area. Its striking whitewashed brick façade is marked by a generous balcony with tall Ionic columns, wrought-iron railing and a graceful arched portico entrance.

One of the most striking features in the East Wing is the sweeping Queen's Staircase, which has been a focal point for generations of visitors. The spiral staircase is so named because Queen Elizabeth II was photographed while descending it on her way to dinner. She and Prince Philip stayed at the inn when they visited Williamsburg in 1957, in honor of the 350th anniversary of the settlement of Jamestown.

The guestrooms offer insight into its "who's who" guest register, which is sprinkled with the names of royalty, heads of state and celebrities from all over the world. Some rooms have framed photos of famous guests who have stayed at the inn, including General Dwight Eisenhower, Sir Winston Churchill, Emperor Hirohito of Japan, Shirley Temple, Bill Cosby, Tom Selleck, Jane Pauley and Garry Trudeau, Al Roker, Willard Scott and Paula Zahn, to name a few.

In 1983, the inn was the site of the International Summit of Industrialized Nations. Hosted by President Ronald Reagan, the summit brought together eight world leaders: Prime Minister Pierre Trudeau of Canada, Chancellor Helmut Kohl of Germany, President Francois Mitterrand of France, Prime Minister Yasuhiro Nakasone of Japan, Prime Minister Margaret Thatcher of Great Britain, Prime Minister Amintore Fanfani of Italy and President Gaston Thorn of the European Community.

Williamsburg Inn

136 East Francis Street

Williamsburg, Virginia 23185

(757) 220-7978

www.colonialwilliamsburg.com

Photographs courtesy of The Colonial Williamsburg Foundation

In 2001, the inn underwent a meticulous renovation. An accomplished team of architects, craftsmen and artisans kept in mind Rockefeller's vision, and the inn's rich history and strong sense of place throughout the process, bringing refreshed vibrancy and elegance to the comfortable Virginia country estate. The number of guestrooms was reduced from 100 to 62, allowing the rooms themselves and bathrooms to be significantly enlarged.

One of the inn's most serene spaces is the Regency Room, the dining room in the West Wing. Incorporating period design elements from the Royal Pavilion at Brighton, England, details include palm-leafed columns, rich silk draperies, leather-upholstered furniture and hand-painted wall panels.

The food is as impressive as the décor. Featuring classic American cuisine with traditional European roots, the menu changes seasonally and includes a nightly local seafood selection. Some of the house specialties are Châteaubriand, Crab Randolph, Queen's Scallops and Grilled Gulf Shrimp. The all-time dessert favorite is Williamsburg Inn Hazelnut Ice Cream Cake with Marinated Strawberries and Kahlúa Fudge Sauce.

Fantastic food and luxurious lodgings in historical surroundings ... the Williamsburg Inn has it all.

CRAB RANDOLPH

One of the Regency Room's specialties, this dish features jumbo lump crab with Virginia ham, crispy flatbread, wilted spinach and a Dijon sauce.

Serves 1

Flatbread

¼ cup all-purpose flour

¼ cup semolina

Water

Olive oil

Sauce Dijonnaise

2 egg yolks

¼ pound clarified butter

1 teaspoon Dijon mustard

Salt and pepper

Crab and Spinach

4 ounces jumbo lump crabmeat

2 tablespoons butter, *divided*

1 shallot, minced, *divided*

1 clove garlic, minced, *divided*

Salt and pepper

2 ounces fresh spinach

1 ounce thinly sliced Virginia ham

In a bowl, combine the all-purpose flour and semolina. Add enough water to form a dough. Roll out paper-thin. Place on a parchment-lined baking sheet. Rub with olive oil. Bake at 350° until crisp.

For the sauce, whisk egg yolks over a double boiler until thick. Remove from the heat. Slowly whisk in butter in a slow stream. Add mustard, salt and pepper.

In a skillet, sauté crabmeat in 1 tablespoon butter with half of the shallot and garlic. Season with salt and pepper. Sauté spinach with remaining butter, shallot and garlic. Season to taste.

To serve, place sautéed spinach in center of plate. Top with flatbread and Virginia ham. Place sautéed crabmeat over ham. Spoon Dijonnaise sauce on top and flash under broiler. Garnish with chive sticks, tomato concassé, reduced balsamic vinegar and brunoise red onion.

Note: Sautéed crabmeat can be placed in a ring cutter on top of the ham to form a cylinder, then remove the ring.

WHITE CHOCOLATE
CROISSANT BREAD PUDDING

Serves 12

1 pound plus 1¹⁄₂ ounces cut-up croissants, baked

5 ounces white baking chocolate *or* couverture

3 cups milk

8 eggs

3 cups heavy whipping cream

6 tablespoons butter, melted

2 ounces crème de cacao

1¹⁄₂ teaspoons vanilla extract

1 cup sugar

¹⁄₂ teaspoon cinnamon

Grease a 13-inch x 9-inch baking dish with nonstick cooking spray; coat with sugar. Fill dish with croissants. Place white chocolate in a large bowl. Heat milk to a boil and pour over the chocolate; stir until melted. Add the remaining ingredients; mix well. Pour over croissants, being sure to coat well.

Let the liquid absorb some before baking (may be prepared the day before). Bake in a water bath at 350° for 45–60 minutes or until firm.

THE MIDWEST

Illinois, Indiana, Iowa, Kentucky, Michigan, Minnesota, Missouri, Ohio and Wisconsin. From the Great Lakes to the headwaters of the mighty Mississippi River, this region offers a wide variety of tourist options. From bustling cities like St. Louis and Chicago to the surrounding farmlands, there is much to stop and see even if you're just driving through from coast to coast.

The Cincinnatian Hotel

The Cincinnatian Hotel

601 Vine Street

Cincinnati, Ohio 45202

(513) 381-3000

(800) 942-9000

www.cincinnatianhotel.com

Built in 1882, the Cincinnatian Hotel was designed as a grand hotel of the 19th century. Originally named the Palace Hotel, this eight-story French Second Empire hotel was the tallest building in Cincinnati. It offered 300 guestrooms and a shared bathroom at either end of each corridor.

As the very best hotel in the city, the Palace was proud to provide elevators and incandescent lighting. It also had hitching posts out front and was strategically located in the heart of the city where the trolley cars made their turns. The Cricket was the only restaurant in the hotel at the time, and it remains popular today.

The hotel's name was changed in the early 1950s. Unfortunately, the quality of the property deteriorated over the next 30 years, and it was about to be torn down to make way for a parking garage. Instead, the hotel closed for 4 years of renovation and, $25 million later, it reopened in 1987 as the grand hotel it is now.

A beautiful atrium topped with a vast skylight was added, and the number of guestrooms was reduced from 300 to 146, including eight suites. The rooms are more spacious and have private baths. The extensive renovation, however, maintained the original flavor of the Palace Hotel in the exterior façade with its mansard roof, and the striking marble and walnut staircase.

The original safe was also kept, and it's now on display in the Cricket Lounge.

Known for its relaxed elegance, the Cricket Lounge kept its original name. The current fine dining room, named the Palace Restaurant, still attracts the discriminating gourmet. The four second-floor meeting rooms reflect the names of the founding fathers of Cincinnati—Filson, Denman, Ludlow and Symmes. The St. Clair Room was named after the individual who, as governor of the Northwest Territory, renamed the city of Losantaville to the city of Cincinnati.

The three major suites also have historical significance: The Emery-Presidential Suite was named for the original owners of the hotel (Thomas and Joseph Emery), the Hannaford Suite for its architect (Samuel Hannaford) and the Briggs Suite for the first general manager (Joseph Briggs). The Maria Nichols Room was named after the woman who founded Rookwood Pottery in Cincinnati in 1880.

Traditional in atmosphere and service, the Cincinnatian captures the warmth and gracious artistry of the turn of the century. Modern amenities and conveniences add comfort and style. The hotel is listed on the National Register of Historic Places and remains the only small luxury hotel in the city.

BANANA CAKES
WITH CARAMEL MASCARPONE

Serves 24

1½ cups all-purpose flour
1 teaspoon baking soda
¼ teaspoon salt
½ cup butter, softened
1 cup sugar
1 teaspoon vanilla extract
2 eggs, beaten
½ cup mashed banana
⅔ cup sour cream

Caramel Mascarpone

2½ cups sugar
2½ cups heavy whipping cream, *divided*
1 pound mascarpone cheese

Sift together the dry ingredients. In a mixing bowl, cream the butter, sugar and vanilla. Slowly beat in eggs and banana.

Alternately add dry ingredients with sour cream. Portion into 24 muffin cups or individual-sized cake pans. Bake at 350° for 40 minutes or until a toothpick comes out clean. Cool for 10 minutes before removing from pans to wire racks.

For the mascarpone, cook the sugar in a heavy saucepan until dark caramel in color. Add 1½ cups cream; stir until smooth. Transfer to a mixing bowl; chill. Add the cheese and remaining cream; mix until combined and whip to medium texture. Chill.

To serve, spoon caramel mascarpone over banana cakes. Arrange fresh figs or other fresh fruit around the mascarpone. Set the cake atop a halved caramelized banana. Garnish top with spun sugar.

PAN-SEARED DIVER SCALLOPS
ON BROCCOLI MOUSSELINE WITH VANILLA INFUSION

Serves 1

6 ounces broccoli crown

2 tablespoons hazelnut oil

6 tablespoons extra virgin olive oil, *divided*

Salt and freshly ground black pepper to taste

¹/₄ cup white wine

1 piece shallot, sliced

¹/₄ piece vanilla bean (Tahitian *or* Madagascar)

2 teaspoons heavy whipping cream

¹/₂ cup butter, *divided*

4 large fresh Maine scallops

In a saucepan, bring salted water to a boil. When the water boils for the second time, add broccoli and cook until tender; drain. Purée broccoli in a blender or food processor; add hazelnut oil and 1 tablespoon olive oil. Season with salt and pepper. Keep warm.

In a medium saucepan, heat wine and shallot until reduced to a syrupy consistency. Add the vanilla bean and cream; let infuse for 10 minutes. Remove from the heat. Mix in 6 tablespoons butter. Strain through a sieve; discard shallot and vanilla bean. Set sauce aside.

In a large skillet, heat remaining olive oil and butter until hot. Pan-sear the scallops on both sides until opaque. Spoon warm broccoli mousse onto a plate; top with scallops and drizzle with sauce. Serve warm.

"The word 'restaurant' evolved from the word 'restore.' If we can restore the guests at the end of the day, not just their body with food, but also their soul with conversation, comfort and humor, then we have succeeded."
    —JoAnn Clevenger, Upperline Restaurant, New Orleans

French Lick Springs Resort

French Lick Springs Resort

8670 West State Road 56

French Lick, Indiana 47432

(812) 936-9300

www.frenchlick.com

The area called French Lick, Indiana, site of the French Lick Springs Resort, was one of the earliest outposts in the middle-Western wilderness. After the discovery of rich mineral springs, which attracted animals that flocked to lick the waters and wet rocks, this valley became known as "The Lick."

The French traders who settled the area had ideas about exploiting the plentiful salt deposits, but because of one obstacle after another, they never made much progress. When Napoleon relinquished claims on that part of the frontier, in the Louisiana Purchase Treaty of 1803, the French abandoned their trading posts.

British settlers moved in around 1812 and succeeded in establishing a permanent fort at The Lick, despite resistance from the Indians. One of the first recorded incidents was the slaying of Irishman William Charles, who was attacked outside the fort. His remains are rumored to be buried somewhere beneath the front lawn of the resort.

The land surrounding the mineral springs, which had been reserved for production of salt, was offered for public sale in 1832. Dr. William A. Bowles (who helped charter the town of French Lick) purchased about 1,500 acres, including all of the large springs, and within several years, he opened the first French Lick Springs Hotel.

It was a ramshackle, three-story frame building, but it was an immediate success because people flocked from hundreds of miles away to partake of the "miracle waters" and to take some water back home with them.

The hotel thrived under various managements until 1897, when a fire destroyed most of the old frame buildings. Not long after, a group calling itself the French Lick Springs Hotel Company purchased the ruins. Irish immigrant Thomas Taggart, who was mayor of Indianapolis at the time, headed the syndicate.

French Lick Springs attained international prominence, thanks to Taggart's strong leadership and imaginative ideas. He rebuilt a new main wing (and later added three more wings) ... had the railroad lay a special spur and run daily trains between Chicago and the hotel's front entrance ... and began bottling the mineral waters for national distribution.

He also modernized and expanded the baths. With the new luxurious spa, the wealthy and elite of society suddenly "discovered" French Lick Springs. Each spring and fall, they came to take "the cure," to play, to conduct business and to gamble (although Taggart always disclaimed any connection with the plush gambling casinos in operation throughout the valley).

Taggart, who was named Democratic National Chairman in 1094 and served briefly as a U.S. Senator by appointment, liked to say he was a hotelman first and political hobbyist second. But his political clout was such that he became the acknowledged power behind Democratic politics in the United States, and French

Lick Springs became the unofficial party headquarters. At a Democratic governors' conference at the resort in 1931, Franklin Roosevelt gathered support for his party's presidential nomination.

After Taggart died in 1929, his son, Thomas D. Taggart, the only boy among six children, carried on. With the Depression, the popularity of French Lick Springs began to decline. World War II brought a momentary revival, but in 1946, young Tom sold out to a New York syndicate.

Today, French Lick Springs Resort features 470 guestrooms, two superb golf courses and numerous other activities on over 2,000 acres, situated in the beautiful Hoosier National Forest. Newly acquired by Boykin Lodging Company, the facility eagerly embraces a new beginning.

Its colorful history includes such honored guests as John Barrymore, Clark Gable, Bing Crosby, President Roosevelt, the Trumans and the Reagans. They walked in the rose gardens, they drank brandy on the veranda and they relaxed in the mineral springs. And now ... you can, too.

TOMATO JUICE

French Lick Springs was the birthplace of tomato juice. The story goes that in 1917, a breakfast order for orange juice couldn't be filled due to short supplies. Chef Louis Perrin came to the rescue with a hastily prepared glass of tomato juice. The concoction was well received by the guests and became a tradition.

At the time, tomato juice wasn't on the commercial market. The demand became so great for this new beverage that the hotel kitchen was turned into a small factory until the process was contracted out to the Tomato Products Company of Paoli, Indiana. Commercially canned tomato juice first appeared for sale in 1928 as a direct result of the favorable reception it received at French Lick Springs.

1/4 bushel ripe tomatoes
1 quart water
2 tablespoons sugar
1 teaspoon salt

Wash and remove stems from tomatoes. Purée or mash through a fine sieve; discard the pulp. To 1 gallon of raw tomato juice, add water, sugar and salt; stir well. Place in the top of a double boiler and heat over boiling water for 30 minutes. Cool slowly and remove to reasonably cool storage. Serve hot or cold.

FRENCH LICK STEAK SOUP

Serves 12
1 cup diced onion
1/2 cup diced celery
1/2 cup diced carrot
1 teaspoon minced garlic
1/4 cup olive oil
2 New York strip *or* rib-eye steaks (12 to 14 ounces *each*), grilled, trimmed and cubed
3 quarts beef stock

1 can (14 1/2 ounces) diced tomatoes
2 teaspoons fresh thyme leaves
Salt and black pepper to taste

In a large saucepan or soup pot, sweat the onion, celery, carrot and garlic in oil. Add steak, stock, tomatoes and thyme. Simmer for at least 2 hours. Season with salt and pepper.

BURGUNDY MUSHROOM SAUCE

Makes about 6 cups

1 pound plus 1 tablespoon butter, *divided*

1 cup all-purpose flour

1 pound button mushrooms

1 teaspoon minced garlic

1 teaspoon cracked pepper

1½ cups Burgundy

2 cups beef stock

Salt and pepper

For roux, in a saucepan, melt 1 pound of butter; stir in flour and cook until smooth. Meanwhile, in another pan, sauté the mushrooms and garlic in remaining butter until tender. Add pepper and Burgundy; bring to a boil and cook until reduced by one-third. Add stock. Season to taste with salt and pepper. Thicken to desired consistency with roux; simmer for 5–10 minutes before serving.

Add an elegant touch to steaks or beef tenderloin with this savory sauce.

Grand Hotel

Grand Hotel

Mackinac Island, Michigan

  49757

(906) 847-3331

(800) 334-7263

www.grandhotel.com

Located in the center of the Great Lakes waterway, Mackinac Island served as a tribal gathering place for the local Native Americans as well as a burial site for their chiefs. Thinking the island resembled a turtle's back, they named it *Michilimackinac,* or "Land of the Great Turtle." Hunters and anglers would meet, trade and rejoin their families while elders discussed tribal affairs.

Mackinac's rich natural bounty attracted both French traders and Jesuit missionaries. Their attraction was so great that the British purchased the island from the local Chippewa in 1781, shortly before the end of the American Revolutionary War. The island remained a battleground during the War of 1812. Once defeated, the British were forced to turn Mackinac over to the Americans. It soon became one of the most valuable trading posts in John Jacob Astor's American Fur Company.

Mackinac's fishing industry quickly overtook fur trading, but then declined due to the rail transportation available to the fishing industry on the mainland. This railroad interest would eventually spawn the Grand Hotel.

In the late 1800s, the island became a popular resort destination, and the local business switched to tourism. In 1875, Congress created Mackinac Island National Park, the country's second national park (after Yellowstone). Mackinac Island National Park became Michigan's first state park in 1895, and it now covers more than 80 percent of the island.

In the 1880s, Mackinac changed greatly. The island's popularity grew, but accommodations were limited. The Michigan Central Railroad, Grand Rapids and Indiana Railroad, and Detroit and Cleveland Steamship Navigation Company formed the Mackinac Island Hotel Company. Within four short months, the Grand Hotel opened as a summer retreat for vacationers, who arrived by lake steamer from Chicago, Erie, Montreal and Detroit, and by rail from across the continent. Rates were $3 to $5 a night for a room ... but a lecture by Mark Twain only cost a dollar.

At 660 feet, the hotel's front porch is the longest in the world. It quickly became the principal meeting place for all of Mackinac. The West Wing was added to the hotel in 1897, inviting even more travelers.

Room rates were $6 a day per person in 1919 when W. Stewart Woodfill was hired as a desk clerk. By 1933, he would purchase the hotel and become the sole owner. He added a radio salon, where patrons could listen to Jack Benny and other programs.

Hollywood's attention brought a film crew to the Grand Hotel, where *This Time for Keeps,* starring Jimmy Durante and Esther Williams, was filmed in 1949. The hotel pool was later named after Ms. Williams.

In 1979, Woodfill sold the hotel to Dan and Amelia Musser, who began a major redesign of the interior and exterior with the help of architect Richard Bos and decorator Carleton Varney. Their efforts once again attracted Hollywood, and *Somewhere*

in Time, starring Christopher Reeve, Jane Seymour and Christopher Plummer, was filmed at the Grand Hotel. Fans of the movie still meet there every October.

Later additions included the Cupola Bar, the Woodfill Conference Center, the East Wing, the Millennium Wing and nine new holes (called the Woods) on the golf course. Combined with the original Grand nine, golfers can now play the Jewel.

Five new rooms—named in honor of First Ladies Barbara Bush, Lady Bird Johnson, Betty Ford, Rosalynn Carter and Nancy Reagan—were recently added to the West End. A full breakfast and five-course dinner are included in the room rates.

The U.S. Department of Interior has designated the Grand Hotel a National Historic Landmark.

Getting to Mackinac Island is half the fun! No cars are allowed on the island. By air, guests can fly commercial, chartered Grand Hotel aircraft, or land their own private and charter aircraft at the Mackinac Island Airport. From May to November, ferries depart from Mackinaw City (on Michigan's Lower Peninsula) or St. Ignace (on the Upper Peninsula), offering frequent crossings throughout the day. It's a short walk from the ferry docks to the Grand Hotel.

CHILLED GREEN APPLE SOUP

Serves 4

10 Granny Smith apples, peeled and cored

1 quart apple juice

$1/2$ cup Riesling

1 cup sugar

1 cinnamon stick

2 tablespoons chopped fresh ginger

2 whole cloves

$1/2$ cup honey

2 tablespoons apple Schnapps

1 cup heavy whipping cream

In a large saucepan or soup pot, combine the apples, juice, wine, sugar, cinnamon, ginger and cloves. Simmer until the apples are very soft. Remove from the heat; let infuse for about 1 hour.

Discard cinnamon stick and cloves. Pour the apple mixture into a blender. Add honey and Schnapps; blend until smooth. Strain soup into a bowl. Lightly whip cream; fold into soup. Adjust seasonings if needed and serve.

GRAND HOTEL PECAN BALLS
WITH FUDGE SAUCE

More than 50,000 Pecan Balls, the hotel's most popular dessert, are served each season.

Serves 4

3 cups vanilla ice cream

2 cups pecan pieces, toasted and chilled

$1/2$ pound unsalted butter

1 quart heavy whipping cream

4 cups light corn syrup

2 pounds chocolate chips

1 vanilla bean, split and scraped

1 tablespoon crème de cacao

Scoop ice cream into four 6-ounce portions and roll into balls. Coat with pecans. Freeze.

For fudge sauce, in a saucepan, bring butter, cream and corn syrup to a simmer. Remove from the heat. Add chocolate chips, vanilla and crème de cacao; stir until well incorporated. Cool. Remove pecan balls from the freezer before serving to soften; pour fudge sauce over pecan balls.

BUFFALO TENDERLOIN
WITH WILD MUSHROOM SALAD AND BLACKBERRY SAUCE

Serves 3

3 buffalo tenderloin medallions (2 ounces *each*)

Salt and pepper

Wild Mushroom Salad

1 shallot, diced

1 clove garlic, minced

1 tablespoon butter

$^1/_3$ cup *each* shiitake, crimini and morel
  mushrooms

1 teaspoon curry powder

1 tablespoon chopped fresh tarragon

1 tablespoon chopped fresh parsley

$^1/_3$ cup hazelnut oil

$^1/_3$ cup olive oil

$^1/_3$ cup rice vinegar

Blackberry Sauce

1 tablespoon olive oil

2 shallots, diced

2 tablespoons pickled ginger

1 cup beef stock

3 tablespoons blackberry jam

2 tablespoons soy sauce

2 tablespoons chopped fresh thyme

1 tablespoon tomato paste

$^1/_3$ cup fresh blackberries

Wild Rice with Pecans and Basil

1 tablespoon butter

1 cup cooked wild rice

1 shallot, diced

2 tablespoons chopped pecans

1 tablespoon chopped fresh basil

Season the buffalo medallions with salt and pepper; set aside. For the mushroom salad, in a skillet, sauté shallot and garlic in butter. Add mushrooms, curry powder, tarragon, parsley, and salt and pepper to taste. Add the oils and vinegar. Remove from the heat; pour into a bowl to infuse. Set aside.

For the sauce, heat oil in a saucepan. Sauté shallots and ginger for 1 minute. Add the stock, jam, soy sauce, thyme and tomato paste. Cook until reduced by half. Strain and adjust seasonings. Add blackberries; set aside.

In a sauté pan, heat butter. Stir in the rice, shallot, pecans and basil; heat through. Season with salt and pepper to taste.

Sear buffalo medallions until medium-rare. Serve with mushroom salad, blackberry sauce and wild rice.

The Pfister Hotel

The Pfister Hotel

424 East Wisconsin Avenue

Milwaukee, Wisconsin

   53202

(414) 273-8222

(800) 472-4403

www.pfisterhotel.com

The vision of businessman Guido Pfister and his son Charles, the Pfister opened in 1893 as a "Grand Hotel of the West" and a welcoming and luxurious meeting place. It surely succeeded on both fronts.

It was the most lavish hotel of its time, constructed over a period of nearly four years at a cost of over $1 million, with groundbreaking features such as fire-proofing, electricity throughout the hotel and thermostat controls in every room.

The exterior appearance of the Pfister, a modernized Romanesque, is due to the unusual construction undertaken. A bed of gravel and hard clay was covered by 2 feet of concrete. On this foundation are 70 limestone pyramids 6 feet in height, each covering about 40 square feet at the base. Pillars were then built on these structures, which support the rest of the hotel.

The bottom three floors are constructed of Wauwatosa limestone, with moldings and trim of Indiana limestone. The top five floors are of Milwaukee cream brick with terra-cotta ornaments. Enormous granite columns on Jefferson Street form a portico—or gentleman's balcony—on the second floor. The seventh floor is devoted to dining facilities, while the remaining floors house 200 guestrooms.

Steel framing beneath the stone exterior underscores the strength and durability of this beautiful building. The grand central stairway, with an ornamental iron balustrade, is a reminder of the strength of conviction of the Pfisters, whose dream this hotel still represents.

The Pfister was showing its age in 1962 when it was purchased by Ben Marcus, who vowed to renovate the distinguished hotel to its original beauty. Significant renovations were completed and a new 23-story guestroom tower was added.

The Pfister has hosted some of the world's most celebrated entertainers and dignitaries. The most historic hotel in Wisconsin, it is also a perennial winner of the AAA Four Diamond Award. Its hallowed halls gleam with the largest Victorian art collection of any hotel in the world.

Art lovers also won't want to miss the Milwaukee Art Museum, located on the city's sparkling lakefront. With its signature Burke Brise Soleil—a 217-foot wing-like sun screen, unprecedented in American architecture—designed by renowned architect Santiago Calatrava, the museum itself is a work of art.

SEARED ATLANTIC SALMON

Serves 4

1 pound parsnips, peeled and chopped

2 tablespoons unsalted butter, cubed

Salt and pepper to taste

2 tablespoons olive oil, *divided*

4 Atlantic salmon fillets (6 ounces *each*)

1 fennel bulb, fronds removed

2 leeks (white portion only)

Peppadew Sauce

1 pound Peppadews*

1 cup rice vinegar

$^1/_2$ cup olive oil

Place the parsnips in a saucepan and cover with water. Bring to a boil; cook for 20 minutes. Drain; place the parsnips in a food processor fitted with a steel blade. Pulse until smooth; incorporate the butter. Season with salt and pepper.

Heat 1 tablespoon of oil in an ovenproof skillet. Season the salmon with salt and pepper. Place fillets in the skillet, skin side up, and don't touch them for 3 minutes!

After 3 minutes, turn the fillets over. Bake at 350° for 8–10 minutes.

Slice the fennel and leeks thinly on a bias. In a sauté pan, heat the remaining oil; add fennel and leeks. Season with salt and pepper. Cook and toss the veggies until they are a nice golden brown, about 4 minutes.

For the sauce, place the peppers and vinegar in a blender; purée until smooth. While processing, slowly add oil and blend until combined.

To serve, spoon parsnip purée in the center of the plate; top with the fennel-leek mixture. Place salmon fillet on top. Drizzle sauce around the plate. Garnish with fresh herbs.

*Peppadews are very sweet peppers— actually classified as a fruit—that can be found at specialty stores or by mail order (www.peppadewusa.com). If you cannot find them, you can substitute roasted red peppers; just add 1 teaspoon of sugar to the mix. Store the sauce in a squeeze bottle and use as a dipping sauce for fish, chicken or pork.

BANANA CREAM PIE

Hazelnut Cookies

1 cup hazelnuts

$^1\!/_2$ cup butter, softened

$^1\!/_4$ cup sugar

1 egg

$^1\!/_2$ teaspoon almond extract

$1^1\!/_2$ cups all-purpose flour

Banana Filling

$^1\!/_4$ cup all-purpose flour

$^1\!/_4$ cup sugar

1 teaspoon salt

1 cup milk

1 egg yolk, beaten

1 banana, mashed

For each serving

1 Hazelnut Cookie

1 banana, peeled

$^1\!/_4$ cup Banana Filling

$^1\!/_2$ cup heavy whipping cream

$^1\!/_2$ teaspoon vanilla extract

1 teaspoon confectioners' sugar

Toast the hazelnuts in a 350° oven for 5 minutes. Transfer to a food processor and finely chop. In a mixing bowl, blend the butter and sugar. Beat in egg and extract. Slowly add flour and chopped nuts; mix until well incorporated. Roll out on a cutting board and cut into desired shapes. Place on a baking sheet. Bake at 350° for 10 minutes.

For filling, combine the flour, sugar and salt in a saucepan. Add milk; simmer over medium heat. Carefully add egg yolk, stirring constantly. Simmer until thick. Stir in banana. Chill for at least 1 hour.

To assemble, place one cookie in the bottom of a cylindrical mold. Slice the banana diagonally into as many pieces as you can; place over cookie in two to three layers, drizzling filling in between.

In a mixing bowl, whip the cream, vanilla and confectioners' sugar until stiff. Spoon over banana slices. To remove from mold, hold it carefully and whack firmly on the counter; let it slide out of the mold onto a plate. Garnish with freshly ground cinnamon or chocolate chips or curls. Drizzle the plate with chocolate sauce.

"Vegetables are a must on a diet. I suggest carrot cake, zucchini bread and pumpkin pie."

—Jim Davis

Saint Paul Hotel

Saint Paul Hotel

350 Market Street

St. Paul, Minnesota 55101

(651) 292-9292

(800) 292-9292

www.stpaulhotel.com

As far back as 1856, John Summers, a contractor by trade, welcomed travelers into his home and later into a 60-room frame hotel—the Greenman House—that he built in 1871. Undaunted by the hotel's destruction by fire in 1877, Summers immediately erected a much bigger and finer hotel, called the Windsor, at a cost of $75,000. Additions to the building were made, and numerous ownership and management changes transpired prior to the hotel's closing in 1906.

In 1908, St. Paul's leading businessmen realized the importance of a luxury hotel to the city's development. Successful entrepreneur Lucius P. Ordway challenged the business community with a pledge of $1 million if the Windsor was razed and the St. Paul Business League would donate the site—Rice Park in the heart of St. Paul— for construction of a new hotel. The challenge was accepted.

Just as they insisted on the finest in construction and materials in the creation of their own mansions overlooking Rice Park, the business leaders were determined that the new building be of exceptional quality and design. The New York firm of Reed and Stem, architects of Grand Central Terminal, was commissioned to create the showcase hotel.

They used brick and stone with a foundation of Indiana limestone to complement the Italian Renaissance Revival design. The street-level windows of the 12-story building featured rounded arches,

accented with sculpted roses and lions adorning the St. Peter Street entrances. Wrought-iron balconies were placed on numerous upper windows. The overall effect was magnificent, stately and dignified.

Proud residents referred to it as "St. Paul's million-dollar hotel." It was called "some of Reed and Stem's finest work" and labeled "an architectural triumph" by a critic of the day.

The Saint Paul Hotel opened with much pomp and ceremony on April 18, 1910. Six thousand American Beauty roses adorned the property. The event was attended by all of the local community leaders, including James J. Hill, builder of the Great Northern Railway, and John Ireland, Archbishop of St. Paul.

Featuring the latest in hotel comforts, it boasted 284 solid porcelain bathtubs and 300 washstands, plus a roof garden, grand ballroom and fine dining room. Every guestroom had a view.

The hotel became the city's center of activity—popular with travelers for its fine guest accommodations, and with local citizens for dining, entertaining and celebrating. President Taft stayed at the Saint Paul during his visit to the Twin Cities. When Congress passed the 19th Amendment in 1919, granting women the right to vote, a celebration was held at the hotel.

In the late 1950s, as life in America changed in focus from city to suburb, the Saint Paul's prominence began to fade. In 1982, a developer began the floor-by-floor,

brick-by-brick restoration of the hotel. The main entrance was moved to the Market Street side of the building, and a former parking lot was transformed into a beautiful new entryway with a sweeping circular drive. Inside, everything was replaced, with the exception of the lobby's three crystal chandeliers, which were restored.

The glitter of those restored chandeliers and a 1925 Italian neoclassic concierge desk give a glimpse back to the hotel's past and add an elegant atmosphere. Each of the 254 guestrooms and suites reflects the European charm of the Saint Paul's golden era, when a legion of notable guests made it their choice of places to stay.

CHICKEN POT PIE

Serves 8

Broth

1 whole chicken

6 cups chicken broth

3 celery ribs, cut into 1-inch pieces

1 carrot, chopped

1 large onion, chopped

2 tablespoons butter

2 to 3 black peppercorns

1 sprig thyme

1 bay leaf

Base

³/₄ cup clarified butter, *divided*

¹/₂ cup plus 1 tablespoon all-purpose flour,
  divided

2 cups diced onions

1¹/₂ cups diced carrots

1¹/₄ cups diced celery

1 cup quartered fresh mushrooms

³/₄ cup white wine

1 cup heavy whipping cream

1 bay leaf

¹/₄ bunch fresh parsley

¹/₂ teaspoon kosher salt

¹/₄ teaspoon black pepper

2 tablespoons liquid egg

2 tablespoons milk

Puff pastry sheets

Place the broth ingredients in a 4-quart stockpot. Bring to a slow boil; reduce heat and simmer for 1–2 hours or until chicken is tender and falls off the bone. Remove chicken and set aside; strain broth and set aside.

For roux, in a small sauté pan, heat ¹/₂ cup butter. Add ¹/₂ cup flour and stir to form a paste. Cook over medium heat, stirring to avoid burning. (Roux should stay light tan in color and will have a nutty taste when done.)

In a heavy 5-quart saucepan over moderate heat, bring remaining butter to the smoking point. Sweat onions until translucent, about 4 minutes. Add carrots; sweat for 2 minutes. Add celery; sweat for 2 minutes. Add mushrooms; heat through. Dust with remaining flour and stir in evenly. Add wine and cook until evaporated. Add 6 cups reserved broth. Bring to a slow boil; reduce to a simmer. Add cream, bay leaf, parsley, salt and pepper. Return to a simmer.

Temper roux with 6–8 ounces of simmering broth from saucepan. Slowly add back to the base, stirring constantly. Cook for 20 minutes or until roux is cooked out.

Pull or shred the poached chicken. Beat liquid egg and milk for egg wash. Cut puff pastry into eight 6- to 8-inch circles (depending on the size of soufflé dishes you are using). Ladle 6 ounces of base into 10-ounce soufflé dishes; add 4 ounces of chicken meat. Brush pastry circles and edge of dishes with egg wash; place pastry over filling and press to seal. Bake at 400° for 15–20 minutes or until puffed and golden brown and internal temperature reaches 165°. Serve immediately.

CREAM OF MINNESOTA
WILD RICE SOUP

Makes 2–3 gallons

1¹/₂ pounds long grain wild rice

¹/₂ pound bacon, finely diced

6 tablespoons clarified butter

1 pound celery, minced

1 pound carrots, minced

1 pound onions, diced

1 pound fresh mushrooms, sliced

¹/₄ cup diced pimientos

2 bay leaves

2 to 3 thyme leaves

1 teaspoon marjoram

Salt to taste

3 teaspoons black pepper

¹/₂ cup sherry

3 cups all-purpose flour

1¹/₂ gallons rich chicken stock

1 quart heavy whipping cream

In a large saucepan, bring 1½ quarts water to a boil. Add wild rice; cover and simmer for 20 minutes (to precook). Meanwhile, in a heavy stockpot, render bacon until crispy. Add butter, celery, carrots and onions; sweat until tender. Add mushrooms and pimientos; cook until tender. Add bay leaves, thyme, marjoram, salt, pepper and sherry. Cook for 20 minutes.

Add wild rice. Stir in flour and blend well; cook for 15 minutes, being careful not to brown. In a large kettle, heat chicken stock to a simmer. After the stock is hot, start adding it to the vegetables. After all of the stock is added, bring soup to a slow boil and simmer. Add cream. Season to taste. Simmer for 1 hour before serving.

"Anybody can make you enjoy the first bite of a dish, but only a real chef can make you enjoy the last."
—François Minot

THE SOUTH

Alabama, Arkansas, Florida, Georgia, Louisiana, Mississippi, South Carolina and Tennessee. With miles and miles of sandy beach along its shores, the South offers extraordinary vacation opportunities. Combined with the mountains of Tennessee, the mega-destinations of Orlando and Disney World, and the city best known for food in the USA (New Orleans), this region offers tourists and residents alike a wide variety of dining choices.

Arnaud's

A fixture in New Orleans' French Quarter since 1918, this popular establishment has a very colorful history.

Arnaud Cazenave was a French wine salesman who based his restaurant business on his belief that the pursuit of the pleasures of the table is as worthy as anything else one does in life. This concept played well to celebration-minded New Orleans, which took Count Arnaud (as he came to be called, without any bona fide claim to the title) to its heart.

Arnaud's was profitable, allowing the Count to expand. He bought up one adjoining property after another until he owned 13 buildings covering most of the block. He constructed an enormous, well-equipped kitchen—still the largest of any freestanding New Orleans restaurant.

He built subsidiary dining rooms throughout the complex, ranging in size from the grand second-floor ballroom to small chambers suitable for secret assignations. Stories about what went on at Arnaud's were the subject of gossip for years. Many of the tales concern the Count's various circumventions of Prohibition.

It was his misfortune to have opened a restaurant the year before the Volstead Act went through. Arnaud believed wine and spirits were natural companions of good food, and the fact that they were illegal seemed a detail.

When the law caught up with him, he was imprisoned and the restaurant padlocked. The Count won the jury over with a convincing explanation of his philosophy and was acquitted in time for the end of Prohibition. He turned his infamy into promotion, and the golden age of Arnaud's was under way.

In the '30s and '40s, Arnaud's was the undisputed leading restaurant of New Orleans and the place to be for any occasion that demanded celebration. Its menu, which defined French-Creole cuisine for decades, was vast.

The restaurant was still in its prime after World War II, when New Orleans became one of the great travel destinations in the west. The excitement and unique culture of the French Quarter drew the most interesting and sophisticated travelers. Unfortunately, the Count's health was declining, and he died a month shy of his 72nd birthday in 1948. A large oil painting of him hangs in the main dining room to this day.

As was his wish, his daughter, Germaine, continued the business. Many doubted her ability to run a restaurant as large and complicated as Arnaud's. But, fueled by a passion to maintain the reputation of her father's masterpiece, she learned the business inside and out. And, even though her management style was unusual, she ran the restaurant with a strong hand for years.

Germaine had a way of attracting attention, and she loved the spotlight, so it's not surprising that her main achievement was in spreading the fame of Arnaud's around the world. Her greatest public-relations triumphs had Arnaud's included among

Arnaud's

813 Rue Bienville

New Orleans, Louisiana 70112

(866) 230-8895

www.arnauds.com

lists of the world's five greatest restaurants—first in a Paris newspaper, then in a celebration of the 2,000th birthday of Paris held in New York. To Germaine, the inclusion was natural. "After all," she said, "New Orleans is the Paris of the South."

Germaine maintained in her mind the image of Arnaud's as a great restaurant, but the threat of impending financial ruin forced her to lease the property. She chose a man named Archie Casbarian to take over, not because of his reputation as one of America's best hoteliers, but based on some coincidences that appealed to her sense of drama: Archie Casbarian had the same initials as her father. Both men loved good cigars, handsome clothes, fine wines and telling an amusing story. Both were born overseas and spoke French fluently. Germaine even thought Archie looked like her father.

Nonetheless, her decision was a good one for the future of the restaurant, which sorely needed Casbarian's creativity and managerial skill. Almost all of the dining rooms had long been closed and were in dire need of repair. Despite that, Casbarian was committed to the idea that the new Arnaud's should look like Arnaud's, not like a brand-new restaurant. The original cypress paneling, chandeliers and iron columns were kept, as were the old ceiling fans, even though few of them worked, then or now.

A small section of the original tin ceiling was found and replicated to cover the entire main dining room. Silver, glassware and china patterns were discovered to be the same as those originally chosen by the Count back in 1918.

Most importantly, the original small Italian tiles that covered the floors throughout the restaurant, changing from building to building—different patterns and colors in every room—were left as they were. In the collective consciousness of New Orleans, tile floors are to Arnaud's what the streetcar is to St. Charles Avenue.

In February of 1979, the renovated dining room reopened, and a long renaissance of Arnaud's began. While new dishes have been added to the menu over the years, they must fit in with the full-flavored Creole cuisine for which Arnaud's is celebrated and New Orleans is known for.

The rich local food supply, particularly fresh seafood, is also key to Creole cooking. Oysters, shrimp, crab and crawfish are featured prominently on Arnaud's menu ... and the style set by the Count almost 90 years ago still inspires everything done to this day.

EGGPLANT CAVIAR APPETIZER

Serves 6

5 medium eggplant
1 cup olive oil
5 tomatoes
1 cup finely diced red onion
1 cup sliced green onions
1 cup lemon juice
$^1/_2$ cup chopped fresh basil
1 tablespoon chopped garlic
Kosher salt and ground white pepper to taste

Brush eggplant with olive oil; place in a shallow baking pan. Bake at 400° for 25 minutes or until very soft. Meanwhile, plunge tomatoes briefly in boiling water to loosen skin. Remove skin and seeds; flatten and chop tomatoes. Set aside.

When baked eggplant is cool enough to handle, cut in half and remove as many seeds as possible (a spoon works well). Scrape the pulp from the skin and dice medium fine. Place in a glass mixing bowl. Add tomatoes, red onion, green onions, lemon juice, basil and garlic. Season with salt and pepper. Refrigerate for at least 30 minutes. Adjust salt and pepper if necessary. Serve with warm toast rounds.

CARAMEL CUSTARD

Serves 6

$^3/_4$ cup sugar, *divided*
1 tablespoon water
3 eggs
2 cups milk, scalded
$^1/_2$ teaspoon best-quality pure vanilla extract

In a small heavy skillet over low heat, stir $^1/_2$ cup sugar and water until the sugar melts, is free of lumps and turns a light caramel color. Pour into six 4-ounce custard cups; let stand until cooled. In a mixing bowl, beat eggs and remaining sugar. Slowly stir in scalded milk. Add vanilla. Strain carefully into the prepared cups to avoid disturbing the caramel.

Place cups in a pan filled with hot water (the water should come almost to the top of the cups). Cover with foil. Bake at 275° for 1½ to 1¾ hours or until a knife inserted in the center comes out clean. Remove cups from the water and cool. Chill. To serve, run a knife around edge of custard and invert the cup onto a small plate.

The Biltmore Hotel

The Biltmore Hotel

1200 Anastasia Avenue

Coral Gables, Florida 33134

(305) 445-1926

(800) 727-1926

www.biltmorehotel.com

As a young man in 1925, George E. Merrick saw the vision of a magnificent hotel on Florida's east coast. He joined forces with Biltmore hotel magnate John McEntee Bowman at the height of the Florida land boom to build a grand hotel.

After 10 months and $10 million, the Biltmore debuted in January 1926 with an inaugural celebration that attracted people from Northern cities on trains marked "Miami Biltmore Specials." Champagne flowed while guests fox-trotted to the sounds of jazz.

This "American Riviera" resort attracted many of the world's rich and famous (and infamous). Bing Crosby, Ginger Rogers, Judy Garland, Al Capone, the Duke and Duchess of Windsor, and assorted Roosevelts and Vanderbilts all stayed there frequently. Fashion shows, gala balls and weddings became routine events. World-class golf tournaments soon followed. Born in the Jazz Age, the hotel often hosted Big Bands to entertain its wealthy, well-traveled visitors.

The Biltmore survived the Depression by offering aquatic galas at its grand pool—these events kept the hotel in the spotlight and drew crowds. Thousands would visit on a Sunday afternoon to enjoy synchronized swimmers, bathing beauties and alligator wrestling. High-diving star Jackie Ott performed from an 85-foot platform. Before making a name for himself in Hollywood, Johnny Weissmuller broke a world record at the Biltmore pool, where he also served as a swimming instructor.

As with several large hotels in America during World War II, the War Department converted the Biltmore to a hospital. It served the wounded as the Army Air Forces Regional Hospital. They sealed many of the windows with concrete and covered the marble floors with linoleum. This early encounter with medicine evolved after the war as the Biltmore became the site of the University of Miami's School of Medicine. Later, the Biltmore functioned as a VA hospital until 1968.

The City of Coral Gables was granted ownership control of the hotel in 1973, through the Historic Monuments Act and Legacy of Parks program. While local government pondered its future, the Biltmore remained unoccupied for nearly 10 years until the decision was made to restore it. Four years and $55 million later, the Biltmore reopened.

The original builder of the Biltmore, George Merrick also developed the city of Coral Gables. He insisted on designing suburbs with strict building codes. The affluent residential areas are graced with broad planted boulevards, golf courses and stately homes. The beautiful surroundings and moderate tropical weather have attracted a thriving business clientele ... Coral Gables is home to over 150 multinational companies.

Complimentary trolley service is available between the Biltmore and downtown Coral Gables, offering a convenient connection to the myriad of shops, restaurants and businesses located along the famed Miracle Mile.

CRISPY SEARED SEA BASS
WITH WILD BERRY-MANGO SALSA AND PURPLE POTATO PURÉE

Serves 4

Purple Potato Purée

2 pounds purple potatoes, peeled

$^1/_2$ cup butter

1 cup half-and-half cream

Salt and pepper to taste

Sea Bass

4 sea bass fillets (8 ounces *each*), skin removed

Salt and pepper to taste

4 tablespoons grapeseed oil

Wild Berry-Mango Salsa

$^1/_4$ cup *each* fresh raspberries, blackberries and
  blueberries

$^1/_4$ cup chopped fresh strawberries

1 cup diced mango

1 tablespoon minced chives

1 tablespoon rice vinegar

1 tablespoon olive oil

Pinch salt and pepper

Place potatoes in a pot and cover with cold water. Bring to a boil. Simmer until a knife can be easily inserted into the center of potato, about 20 minutes. Drain well.

Press the potatoes through a potato ricer or food mill into a mixing bowl. Add the butter, cream, salt and pepper; mix until incorporated, but do not overmix. Keep warm.

Season the sea bass with salt and pepper on both sides. Heat an ovenproof skillet on high heat; add grapeseed oil and heat just until it begins to smoke. Carefully place the fillets, skin side up, in the pan; sear until golden brown. Remove from the heat. Turn fillets over and place the skillet directly into the oven. Bake at 400° for 7 minutes or until fish is cooked to your desired doneness.

Meanwhile, for salsa, carefully cut the raspberries, blackberries and blueberries in half. Place in a bowl; add the remaining ingredients and stir gently.

To serve, place about ¾ cup purple potato purée on each plate. Top with sea bass; place a spoonful of wild berry-mango salsa over fish. Garnish with any seasonal steamed vegetables.

Blackberry Farm

As the sun rises over the foothills of the Great Smoky Mountains, the morning mist fades to unveil one of America's great hidden treasures, Blackberry Farm. The 4,200-acre mountain haven has been a tranquil escape for family, friends and guests for more than 70 years as it evolved into a luxurious resort of breathtaking scenery, gourmet cuisine and pleasurable pastimes.

In the 1930s, on a trip from Chicago to the Georgia coast, Dave and Florida Laiser were enthralled by the majesty of these mountains and discovered the perfect setting for their dream home. In 1940, while selecting just the right location, Florida snagged her silk stockings in a thicket of blackberry bushes, and the name Blackberry Farm was born.

In 1976, the farm's charm captivated Kreis and Sandy Beall and inspired their own dream. As a new mother of 4-month-old Sam, Kreis made Blackberry the family's home and opened the beautiful property to the public as a six-room country inn. Sam's love for Blackberry began at an early age as he followed his mom around the kitchen while she prepared and served meals and welcomed their first guests. The Bealls' vision for Blackberry Farm became a reality.

Through the years, Blackberry has welcomed guests from the far reaches of the globe as well as nearby neighbors, with the genuine Southern hospitality and personal attention that have become its hallmark. Today, proprietor Sam Beall continues his family's tradition of entertaining by creating and hosting an exciting annual series of cooking schools, wine tastings and epicurean events.

More than 30 years ago, Blackberry Farm was founded on the idea of entertaining with good friends and good food. The mission today is the same, but on a higher gastronomic level. With events such as the 2005 Food and Wine Happenings and the daily culinary experiences, Blackberry is determined to become one of the ultimate food and wine destinations in America.

Blackberry Farm

1471 West Millers Cove Road

Walland, Tennessee 37886

(865) 984-8166

(800) 648-4252

www.blackberryfarm.com

BLACKBERRY GLAZED QUAIL

Serves 10

³/₄ cup Madeira

¹/₂ cup vegetable oil

¹/₄ cup minced shallots

1 teaspoon thyme

¹/₄ teaspoon black pepper

10 semi-boneless quail

Glaze

2 tablespoons chopped sweet onion

1¹/₂ teaspoons chopped garlic

1 tablespoon butter

2 tablespoons sugar

¹/₂ cup blackberry juice

2 tablespoons water

1 tablespoon balsamic vinegar

1¹/₂ teaspoons soy sauce

In a glass container, combine the wine, oil, shallots, thyme and pepper; add quail. Cover and refrigerate overnight.

For glaze, in a saucepan, sweat onion and garlic in butter over medium heat. Add sugar, blackberry juice, water, vinegar and soy sauce. Bring to a simmer. Remove from the heat; cool completely.

Remove quail from marinade; discard marinade. Fold legs of quail so that feet poke into skin at back of breast cavity; place in a baking pan. Brush cooled glaze over quail. Let stand for 2 hours.

Bake at 400° for 8–10 minutes or until quail is cooked to medium, brushing with glaze every 2–3 minutes. Serve atop black-eyed pea salad with roasted squash or crisp Tennessee bacon.

PECAN AND RICE CRUSTED TROUT

Serves 8

8 trout fillets (6 to 8 ounces *each*), skin on

1 cup buttermilk

4 tablespoons hot sauce

1 cup uncooked Uncle Ben's Rice*

2 cups pecans, chopped

1 cup all-purpose flour

Salt and pepper

3 tablespoons clarified butter

Remove pin bones from the fillets. In a shallow bowl, combine buttermilk and hot sauce. In a blender or food processor, blend rice until it becomes slightly coarser than flour. Transfer to a shallow bowl; add pecans and all-purpose flour. Season with salt and pepper.

Heat butter in a large sauté pan. Dip skinless side of trout in the buttermilk mixture, then in the pecan mixture. Gently place fillets, skin side up, in the hot butter. Brown completely, then flip into a clean sauté pan. Finish in oven if necessary (trout will not take long to cook through, so it may cook completely on top of the stove).

You may substitute rice flour for the rice. It will have a finer texture.

HUGUENOT TORTE

Apple Cake

12 ounces pecans

1 cup all-purpose flour, *divided*

6 eggs

2 cups sugar

4 teaspoons baking powder

1 teaspoon salt

$^1/_2$ teaspoon cinnamon

$^1/_2$ teaspoon cardamom

4 Granny Smith apples, peeled and grated

4 teaspoons vanilla extract

Filling

Fig purée

Apple juice

Bourbon Cream

2$^1/_2$ cups heavy whipping cream

2 tablespoons Wild Turkey bourbon

2 tablespoons sugar

1 tablespoon vanilla extract

In a food processor, grind pecans with ¼ cup flour until fine but not oily; set aside.

In a mixing bowl over a double boiler, heat eggs and sugar to 110°. Whip on high speed until eggs triple in volume. (The eggs will fall slightly and be whipping below the "high water mark" on the side of the mixing bowl.)

Sift together the baking powder, salt, cinnamon, cardamom and remaining flour; fold into eggs. Fold in pecans, then apples and vanilla. Pour batter into three greased and parchment-lined 9-inch cake pans. Bake in a 325° convection oven (on low fan) for 35 minutes. Sides will pull away slightly when done. Turn out onto cardboard cake circles, parchment side down.

For filling, reconstitute the fig purée with apple juice and purée again. Spread over one cake layer; top with a second cake layer and remaining filling. Top with third cake layer. In a mixing bowl, beat bourbon cream ingredients; spread over top and sides of cake. Garnish sides with toasted chopped nuts if desired.

Boca Raton Resort & Club

Boca Raton Resort & Club

501 East Camino Real

Boca Raton, Florida 33431

(888) 491-2622

www.bocaresort.com

Addison Mizner, a self-taught architect, moved to Palm Beach in 1918 hoping to improve his health. The flare-up of an old injury and the urging of his friend Paris Singer, heir to the sewing machine fortune, prompted Mizner's move from New York to Florida. Gaining a local reputation as both a builder and an architect, Mizner went on to design and build great mansions for the elite.

Frank Lloyd Wright once said that many architects had imagination, but only Mizner had the courage to let it out of the cage. As his health improved, Mizner ventured south of Palm Beach to Boca Raton. The Florida land boom was in full swing, with mangrove swamps and scrubland giving rise to whole towns. Real estate developers, land speculators and hustlers flocked to the state, hoping to become millionaires by selling pieces of paradise to snowbound Northerners.

Mizner and his brother, Wilson, formed a land development company and acquired 17,500 acres of Boca Raton property. Then Mizner proceeded to design an elegant structure in an imaginative pseudo-Spanish style with courtyards, and furnished it with his private collection of rare antiques from old churches and universities in Spain and Central America.

It cost $1.25 million to build the Cloister Inn, making it the most expensive 100-room hotel ever built at the time. The hotel's luxurious ambience quickly attracted movie stars, royalty and industrialists, including Harold Vanderbilt, George Whitney, Florenz Ziegfeld, Al Jolson and Elizabeth Arden.

Unfortunately, the glory of the Cloister Inn lasted just one season. By the time it opened in February of 1926, the land boom in Florida was already faltering and investors were becoming skeptical of fraudulent developers. Mizner's investors began to withdraw their support. Management of the company was taken over by Rufus Dawes and his brother, Charles (who was Vice President of the United States at the time). The Dawes brothers were unable to rescue the Cloister from bankruptcy, and it succumbed when a hurricane in September 1926 killed nearly 400 people and destroyed many of the "boom time buildings."

In 1928, Clarence Geist, a one-time railway brakeman from Indiana who made a fortune in utilities, bought the assets of the failed corporation. He hired golf course architects to reconstruct the hotel's two courses and proceeded to expand the Cloister Inn. Two years and $8 million later, it opened as the Boca Raton Club, one of the world's finest "gentlemen's clubs."

Though it was never fiscally profitable, an exclusive membership kept the club flourishing. Private railroad cars and yachts brought in such notables as Herbert Hoover, several du Ponts, Jacob Raskob and other celebrities. Geist subsidized the perennial club deficit throughout the Depression and even after his death (via his estate), by which time the property had grown to four times its original size.

During World War II, the ornate pillars and carved plaster pieces were padded, and the elaborate furnishings were stored away to make room for GI bunks when the government commandeered the Boca Raton Club. The Army Air Corps officers housed there referred to their quarters as "the most elegant barracks in history."

After the war, the club was purchased by J. Myer Schine, a hotel, theater and real estate magnate, who paid a mere $3 million for it. Completely refurbished and modernized, the club reopened in 1945 as the Boca Raton Hotel and Club and became extremely popular.

The future of the resort was secured when Arthur Vining Davis (ArViDa), a founder of ALCOA, bought the property for $22.5 million in 1956. It was the biggest real estate deal in Florida history up until then. Arvida Corporation owned the resort until 1983. A series of corporate owners continued expanding and remodeling the property until the current owners paid $1.2 billion for it in December 2004.

Legend has it that Ponce de Leon sailed along the shore of Boca Raton when he discovered Florida in 1513. Tales of Spanish conquistadors, pirates and Indians enrich the mystique of the tropical paradise, which grew from a tiny farm settlement to one of the world's most beautiful resorts. Dreamers, risk-takers, moguls and millionaires all contributed to the creation of Florida's Boca Raton.

The resort retains its share of guests who remember a long-gone era, and it boasts many newcomers, business travelers, couples and families who come to enjoy the resort's unparalleled setting and luxurious accommodations. Heads of state and celebrities such as George Bush, John Travolta, Sylvester Stallone, Bette Midler, Tom Selleck and Oprah Winfrey have been seen here.

Fresh from more than $100 million in renovations, the Boca Raton Resort & Club is one of the country's premier resort destinations and private club facilities. Amenities include a half-mile stretch of private beach, two 18-hole championship golf courses, 30 tennis courts, full-service marina, several pools, state-of-the-art spa and fitness centers, a variety of water sports, a comprehensive children's program and, last but not least, an outstanding selection of dining options.

SMOKED MAHI-MAHI DIP

This flavorful make-ahead dip is perfect for a cocktail party or other occasion when you're hosting a large group.

Makes about 4 cups

1 pound smoked mahi-mahi, ground
6 ounces onion, puréed
1 cup mayonnaise
3 tablespoons sour cream
2 tablespoons horseradish
2 tablespoons lemon juice
1 tablespoon white Worcestershire sauce
1 teaspoon Liquid Smoke, optional

1 teaspoon Tabasco
$^1/_2$ teaspoon dry mustard
$^1/_2$ teaspoon white pepper
$^1/_2$ teaspoon sea salt

In a bowl, combine all ingredients until well blended. Add 1–2 more tablespoons of mayonnaise if needed. Cover and refrigerate for 4 hours before serving.

RISOTTO "SUNNY SIDE UP"
WITH MASCARPONE AND WHITE TRUFFLE OIL

Serves 4

$2^1/_2$ to 3 quarts vegetable *or* chicken stock
4 tablespoons butter
4 tablespoons extra virgin olive oil
3 shallots, finely chopped
2 cups uncooked Arborio rice
$^3/_4$ cup vin santo (Cognac, brandy *or* sherry may be substituted)
4 tablespoons mascarpone
Salt and white pepper to taste
$1^1/_2$ cups shaved Parmigiano-Reggiano cheese (about 4 to 5 ounces)
4 quail eggs, cracked and separated from the whites, yolks reserved
4 tablespoons white truffle oil (available at specialty markets)

In a saucepan, heat the stock to a simmer. Meanwhile, in a separate large, round heavy saucepan, heat the butter and oil over medium heat. Add shallots and sweat for 2 minutes.

Add the rice; cook and stir until coated, about 4 minutes or until it looks toasty.

Add 2 cups of hot stock, but do not stir. Be careful, as the steam rises quickly. Increase heat to medium-high. Add stock every 4–6 minutes in 1- to 2-cup portions, only adding as the rice absorbs the previous amount (the liquid should not pool on top of the risotto). Keep stirring and adding stock.

Taste after 10–13 minutes. If the rice is too hard, keep cooking the risotto, repeating the procedure with adding stock. If the rice tastes al dente, like pasta with a little bite, you are 4 minutes away from finished risotto. At this stage, add the vin santo and simmer for 2 minutes. Fold in the mascarpone and season with salt and white pepper.

Spoon risotto onto four plates. Sprinkle with Parmigiano-Reggiano. Place an egg yolk in the center of risotto. Drizzle each plate liberally with white truffle oil and serve.

1886 Crescent Hotel & Spa

The first account of the history of the 1886 Crescent Hotel & Spa is taken from the *Eureka Springs Times Echo,* one of the city's early newspapers, which is still in existence today:

Crescent Hotel Opens Today—May 20, 1886

"With the opening of the grandiose Crescent Hotel, Eureka Springs entered a new and exciting era. Notables from afar are arriving in our fair city.

"The Crescent, built by the Eureka Springs Improvement Company and The Frisco Railroad, is America's most luxurious resort hotel. Featuring large airy rooms, comfortably furnished, the Crescent Hotel offers the visiting vacationer opulence unmatched in convenience and service.

"Tonight's gala ball will find in attendance many of the leaders in business and society. As guest of honor, the Honorable James G. Blaine, the Republican presidential nominee, will attend with his charming wife, Laura. The very popular Harry Barton and his orchestra will play for the festivities.

"In the Grand Ballroom of the new Crescent, the opening banquet for the 400 celebrants will be followed by a dedication ceremony with the honorable Mr. Blaine as guest speaker."

Another article from the *Times Echo* describes the construction process:
America's Newest and Most Luxurious Hotel Built at a Cost of $294,000—May 20, 1886

"It was two years ago that Powell Clayton and his associates chose the site of the new Crescent Hotel ... 27 acres at the north end of West Mountain, a majestic location overlooking the valley. The commissioning of Isaac Taylor as architect was announced and construction commenced.

"Seldom has such a formidable construction undertaking been accomplished with such efficiency. Special wagons were constructed to transport the huge pieces of magnesium limestone from the quarry site on the White River near Beaver. Due to the density of this special stone, and the precision necessary in cutting and fitting, a group of specialists from Ireland was brought here to assist and advise in construction.

"Mr. O'Shawnessey, spokesman and leader of the group, said throughout the many years of his stoneworking, he has never encountered a stone with such density and quality as the White River Limestone. He predicts it will become a popular building stone in the future and further stated that because of its unique characteristics, the 18-inch-thick walls of the Crescent, fitted without the use of mortar, would withstand the destructive forces of time and retain its original beauty for years to come.

"The magnificent structure was then furnished in the most exquisite manner. It is lighted with Edison lamps, furnished with electric bells, heated with steam and open grates, has a hydraulic elevator and is truly a showplace of today's conveniences."

1886 Crescent Hotel & Spa

75 Prospect Avenue

Eureka Springs, Arkansas

  72632

(479) 253-9766

(877) 342-9766

www.crescent-hotel.com

The Crescent Hotel was originally an exclusive year-round resort catering to the carriage set. During the Victorian years, it was a model of gracious Southern hospitality. Popular activities included horseback riding, afternoon tea dances, evening dance parties, picnics, hiking, streetcar rides and Tallyho rides in a horse-drawn coach.

While always used as a hotel, the Crescent was also a fine women's college during the off-season from 1908 through 1931.

Today, the 1886 Crescent Hotel & Spa is still the place to dine in grand style overlooking downtown Eureka Springs. Guests can tour the magnificent gardens, play darts or billiards in the rooftop game room or even take a ghost tour ... the hotel likes to say it's "America's most haunted resort."

The Crescent is also home to the extraordinary Welte Organ. The "Welte Philharmonic Salon Model 4" is 10½ feet tall, 8 feet wide and 4 feet deep. It has about 250 pipes plus percussion (two drums and a cymbal). The unique organ was made around 1912 in Freiburg, Germany, by M. Welte and Sohne, probably the largest and best-known maker of automatic (self-playing) organs at the time. It is one of three of this model still known to exist.

The Crescent's organ has undergone a full mechanical restoration and still plays on its original 100-note rolls, some of which play one tune while others play five. It's just one thing that makes a visit to this resort worthwhile.

CRAB LORENZO

This dish was served at the hotel's grand opening on May 20, 1886.

Serves 10–12

16 mushrooms, minced
4 shallots, minced
4 cloves garlic, minced
1/2 pound butter
2 cups all-purpose flour
3 quarts half-and-half cream
1 cup white wine
1/4 cup Worcestershire sauce
8 tablespoons chives
4 bay leaves
3 pounds crabmeat
Salt and pepper to taste
Toast points
Chopped parsley and lemon wedges

In a large pot, sauté the mushrooms, shallots and garlic in butter until tender. Slowly mix in flour to make a roux. Add cream, wine and Worcestershire sauce; cook until smooth. Add chives and bay leaves; simmer for 30 minutes, stirring occasionally. Add crabmeat; cook for 5 minutes. Season with salt and pepper.

To serve, place enough toast points to cover the bottom and sides of individual ovenproof ramekins or bowls. Spoon crab mixture over toast and lightly brown top in the oven. Garnish with parsley and lemon.

SOUTHWEST PASTA WITH BLACKENED CHICKEN

Blackening Spice

1 cup black pepper

1 cup salt

3 tablespoons fennel seed, crushed

2 tablespoons dried thyme

2 tablespoons paprika

2 tablespoons ground mustard

2 tablespoons granulated garlic

1 tablespoons cayenne pepper

2 tablespoons dried sage

Southwest Sauce

4 cups salsa

2 cups olive oil

2 cups white Zinfandel

$1/4$ cup Dijon mustard

4 eggs, beaten

2 cups grated Parmesan cheese

2 tablespoons Rose's lime juice

2 tablespoons herb seasoning

For each serving

8 ounces bowtie pasta

1 boneless skinless chicken breast (6 ounces)

Combine the blackening spice ingredients; store in a covered container in a cool dry place.

For the sauce, in a large bowl, combine the salsa, oil, wine, mustard, eggs, Parmesan cheese, lime juice and herb seasoning; add 2 tablespoons blackening spice. Transfer 8 ounces of sauce to a sauté pan; bring to a boil. Reduce heat and simmer until heated through. Refrigerate remaining sauce to make the recipe another time.

Cook the pasta until tender. Meanwhile, rub chicken breast with desired amount of blackening spice; grill until cooked. Drain pasta and add to the sauce; toss until coated. Slice grilled chicken; serve over pasta.

The Delta Queen

What better way to truly experience America's heartland than by cruising on its rivers, as the big red paddlewheels churn and the picturesque scenery glides by? Steamboatin'® on en elegant paddlewheeler is like stepping back in time, when life moved at a slower pace. You can almost imagine what it was like back when this way of travel got its start.

On June 22, 1890, Capt. Gordon Christopher Greene, a newly licensed river pilot, bought a steamboat at an auction on the Cumberland River in Nashville, Tennessee. He formed Greene Line Steamers with that first boat, the *H.K. Bedford*, which he entered into service on the upper Ohio and Kanawha rivers.

Capt. Gordon built a reputation for customer service and delivering what he promised. He successfully merged with some of his rivals, while others that couldn't compete were forced to retire from the river.

The Greene Line expanded as more vessels were added to the fleet, and soon Capt. Gordon, realizing that freight would not sustain the line, expanded his operations to include passengers.

The captain's wife, Mary, stood watch in the pilothouse with him and rapidly learned the river. She became one of the first licensed women riverboat pilots.

After Capt. Gordon passed away in 1927, his family took over the wheel and guided the Greene Line into the stormy days of World War II. With the home front population starved for affordable wartime getaways, overnight Steamboatin' vacations became extremely popular.

The company steamed out of the war years strong and robust. In fact, the *Gordon C. Greene* was often filled to capacity, which meant it was time to find another steamboat. Two of them were found—in California.

The *Delta Queen*® was a river steamer that was part of the Navy's "mothball fleet" near the Sacramento River. It had served gallantly during the war, functioning as a troop carrier and ferryboat in San Francisco Bay. At one point the steamer even served as a floating gun installation, covering Alcatraz during a prisoner uprising.

For a bid of slightly more than $47,000, the Greenes acquired the *Delta Queen* at government auction. They'd found a bargain, but the steamer was thousands of miles away. Under the supervision of Capt. Fred Way, a longtime family friend, the *Delta Queen* was boarded up like a giant piano box and towed down the California coast, through the Panama Canal, across the Gulf of Mexico and up the Mississippi River. Under its own power, it steamed proudly upriver to Cincinnati and then to Pittsburgh, where it underwent a thorough refurbishment.

In 1948, the *Delta Queen* officially joined the Greene Line's fleet and took her place on the Mississippi system. Capt. Mary Greene, affectionately known to river folk as "Ma" Greene, moved into a specially outfitted suite on the Cabin Deck. She passed away several months later, having served 55 years on the river. Shortly thereafter, her daughter-in-law,

The Delta Queen

    Steamboat Co.

Robin Street Wharf

1380 Port of New Orleans

    Place

New Orleans, Louisiana 70130

(504) 586-0631

www.deltaqueen.com

Letha Greene, took over the company.

An economic downturn in the late '50s threatened the company, forcing Mrs. Greene to sell all of the vessels except for the *Delta Queen.* When it appeared she would have to shut down entirely, California businessman Richard Simonton, enamored with his trips on the *Delta Queen,* came to the rescue.

He hired a publicist, Betty Blake, to help revitalize national interest in paddlewheel vacations on the country's heartland rivers. She was so successful that by the mid-1960s, the Greene Line had paid off its entire debt. Then, just as things were looking rosy, Congress passed an American version of the international Safety of Life at Sea (SOLAS) convention. The days of substantially wooden passenger vessels, among them the *Delta Queen,* were numbered.

Blake organized a nationwide "Save the Queen" campaign, and supporters flooded Congress with petitions. Turned out Steamboatin' is a resilient American institution, and the *Delta Queen* continues to operate today under a special congressional exception to SOLAS legislation.

Plans for an all-steel steamboat were being made when the Greene Line was renamed the Delta Queen Steamboat Co. in 1974—the *Mississippi Queen*® was launched during America's bicentennial. In the '80s, the company headquarters were moved to a turn-of-the-century warehouse on the New Orleans riverfront, where the first-ever steamboat passenger terminal was built.

Today, vacationers can choose from a wide variety of river trips on the *Mississippi Queen, American Queen*® (launched in 1995) or their venerable sister, the *Delta Queen,* visiting such historic ports of call as Nashville, Natchez, Hannibal, St. Louis, Chattanooga and Cincinnati. Steamboatin' will continue to keep alive that special rhythm of an American way of life.

BAYOU STUFFED CATFISH
WITH CAJUN BEURRE BLANC

Serves 6

¹/₂ pound jumbo lump crabmeat

1 loaf baked cornbread (6 x 3 x 1 inches), crumbled

1 cup cooked spinach, chopped

¹/₄ cup pine nuts, toasted

1 tablespoon Creole mustard

6 boneless catfish fillets (6 ounces *each*), skin removed

1 cup all-purpose flour

Salt and pepper to taste

1 cup buttermilk

2 cups Zatarain's Fish-Fri mix

Blackened Seasoning

¹/₃ cup paprika

¹/₄ cup salt

1 tablespoon *each* garlic powder and onion powder

1 teaspoon *each* white, black and cayenne pepper

¹/₂ teaspoon *each* dried thyme, basil and oregano

6 ounces butter, cut into 1-inch pieces

¹/₂ cup vegetable oil

Cajun Beurre Blanc

1¹/₂ cups white wine

1 clove garlic, crushed

1 bay leaf

1 teaspoon black peppercorns, cracked

1 lemon, halved

2 shallots, minced

1 cup heavy whipping cream

1 pound butter, cut into 1-inch pieces

Combine the crab, cornbread, spinach, pine nuts and mustard. Spread the mixture over catfish fillets; roll tightly and refrigerate until set. Season flour with salt and pepper. Dredge fillets in flour, dip in buttermilk and coat with mix. Deep-fry at 350° until light brown. Place on a baking sheet. Finish in a 350° oven until internal temperature reaches 150°.

Meanwhile, in a bowl, combine the seasoning ingredients and mix well. Refrigerate until needed. In a heavy saucepan, combine the first six sauce ingredients. Cook over low heat until reduced. Add heavy cream and reduce by half. Slowly add butter, whipping continuously, and alternating pan on and off the heat. Strain; add 1 tablespoon blackened seasoning. Serve with stuffed catfish. Garnish with lemon wedges.

Don CeSar Beach Resort

Don CeSar Beach Resort

3400 Gulf Boulevard

St. Petersburg Beach,

　Florida 33706

(727) 360-1881

(866) 728-2206

www.doncesar.com

Florida's legendary "Pink Palace" opened in 1928 during the Great Gatsby era. Don CeSar Beach Resort was the dream of Irishman Thomas Rowe, who found his fortune in Florida real estate. Constructed on 80 acres (purchased for $100,000) of what would become St. Petersburg Beach, the resort was built to resemble the Royal Hawaiian in Waikiki Beach. At a cost of $1.2 million, it was nearly 300 percent over budget.

Rowe chose the name for his hotel as a nod to the main character in the English opera *Maritana*, Don Caesar de Bazan. Referred to simply as "The Don" by generations of privileged guests from around the world, the luxury resort has been revered internationally for its sprawling, sugar-white beach and great dining.

In its early years, and even during the Depression, it was the hot spot for high society, attracting such notables as F. Scott Fitzgerald, Clarence Darrow, Lou Gehrig and Al Capone. Rates were $30 per day for suites and $14 per day for a single, including meals. Dinner and dancing commanded tuxedos and gowns, and the cost was $2.50 a person.

When the banks failed in 1931, Rowe's savings disappeared and he had nothing left to finance the next season. Colonel Jacob Ruppert came to the rescue and signed a three-year contract to house his New York Yankees at the hotel during spring training. Rowe served the players steak every morning as well as unlimited quantities of milk. The team attracted a satellite of sports writers and family members, which kept the hotel nearly full.

Hard times befell the resort when Rowe died. He hadn't signed his will, in which he intended to leave his "pink lady" to its loyal family of employees, so his estranged wife of 30 years became the reluctant heir. In less than three years, the Don lost much of its personality and charm that had established its prominent standing among resorts.

In 1942, the U.S. Army purchased the property for an "assessed value" of only $450,000 and turned it into a convalescent center for battle-fatigued World War II airmen. St. Petersburg girls formed a group called the "Bomb-a-Dears" to aid the airmen in the resocialization process.

After the war, the Veterans Administration stripped the building for use as a regional office, later moving out in 1967, unable to afford necessary repairs. The abandoned hotel became a graffiti canvas, doomed for the wrecking ball. Fortunately, a diligent preservation group located a buyer who shared Rowe's vision of grandeur.

In 1973, the hotel reopened as a luxury resort with a continued commitment to revitalization, allowing the Don CeSar to reign as the Pink Castle on Florida's Gulf Coast. From September 1985 to January 1989, extensive renovations transformed the ornate Spanish interiors with light woods and fabrics, creating a Continental look.

In 1994, a multimillion-dollar revitalization included a 4,000-square-foot full-service Beach Club and Spa. Other additions were a second outdoor swimming pool surrounded by tropical gardens ... an all-inclusive shopping arena ... expanded function space ... and a signature restaurant, the Maritana Grille, recipient of the AAA Four Diamond rating. In late 1999, the grand entrance and staircase were upgraded with emerald marble and other intricate details.

Don CeSar Beach Resort recently completed a $20 million enhancement project that included a revitalized lobby with rich mahogany accents and vibrant upholsteries, and a grand makeover of guestrooms with custom-made wrought-iron furniture, luxurious bedding and completely renovated bathrooms.

Interiors feature English Axminster carpets, Italian crystal chandeliers, French candelabras and fountains, and works depicting picturesque Florida. International influences are woven through the 277 European-styled guestrooms, including 43

spacious suites. Mediterranean-styled rooms and spacious suites are enhanced by breathtaking views of the Gulf of Mexico or Boca Ciega Bay. Twin, two-story penthouses offer the ultimate in exclusivity with sweeping terraces overlooking shimmering waters.

The Maritana Grille invites guests to plunge into the deep blue. Patrons dine surrounded by 1,500 gallons of salt water and indigenous fish. Delight in New American cuisine, prepared over a pecan and cherrywood grill, and a choice of more than 200 selections of fine wine. The restaurant is open for dinner, and jackets are not required. Sunday brunch in the highly acclaimed King Charles Ballroom combines gourmet masterpieces and spectacular Gulf views with over 180 delicious selections.

Listed on the National Register of Historic Places, Don CeSar Beach Resort continues to charm discriminating guests with gracious service preserved from the Gatsby era of pampering.

VANILLA BEAN MASHED POTATOES

Serves 4

1¹/₂ pounds Yukon Gold potatoes

¹/₄ cup sour cream

7 tablespoons butter

2 tablespoons vanilla extract

1 vanilla bean, scraped

Salt and pepper to taste

Place the potatoes in a large saucepan and cover with water. Bring to a boil; cook until tender. Drain and let rest for 1 minute. In a mixing bowl, combine the sour cream, butter, vanilla extract and vanilla seeds. Press potatoes through a food mill into the bowl; whisk until combined. Season with salt and pepper.

RASPBERRY SOUFFLÉ

Serves 4

12 chilled egg whites
1 1/2 teaspoons cream of tartar
1 1/4 cups confectioners' sugar
1/2 cup raspberry purée
1/4 cup butter
2 tablespoons sugar
1/2 pint fresh raspberries

In a mixer, whip egg whites on high speed for 30-40 seconds. Add cream of tartar and confectioners' sugar. Whip on medium speed until the whites have stiff peaks with good density, volume and shine.

Transfer half of the whites to a stainless steel bowl; slowly fold in raspberry purée. Fold in the remaining whites until incorporated. Lightly butter the inside of four soufflé dishes, using 1 tablespoon for each, and dust each with ½ tablespoon of sugar.

Divide the raspberries among the dishes; spoon in soufflé mixture. Tap the dishes on a hard surface to eliminate any air pockets. Bake at 350° for 14–18 minutes. The soufflés should rise and be firm.

CAVIAR WITH SEMOLINA CROSTINI

1 semolina baguette
1/2 cup butter, softened
1/2 cup minced shallots
4 ounces Beluga caviar
1/2 cup minced chives
1/2 cup crème fraîche
1/2 cup minced cooked egg whites
1/2 cup minced cooked egg yolks

Thinly slice the baguette. Spread a light coat of butter on both sides of each slice. Grill until toasted on both sides. Place some minced shallots on each slice.

Place the caviar in mother-of-pearl spoons; display around the chives, crème fraîche, egg whites and yolks. Serve with crostini.

Jekyll Island Club Hotel

Jekyll Island Club Hotel

371 Riverview Drive

Jekyll Island, Georgia 31527

(912) 635-2600

(800) 535-9547

www.jekyllclub.com

Situated on a Georgia barrier island, Jekyll Island Club Hotel originally served as an exclusive hunting retreat for the nation's most powerful financiers and industrialists of the late 1800s and early 1900s. The hotel today is a unique modern resort with architectural character and a charming historic ambience.

The main structures, built between 1887 and 1902, were designed by Charles Alexander of Chicago and Charles Alling Gifford of New York. Alexander designed the original clubhouse in the American Queen Anne style, incorporating extensive verandas, bay windows, extended chimneys, the turret that dominates the roofline and the overall asymmetrical design.

Handsome interior details include Ionic columns in the dining room, 12- and 15-foot ceilings, oak wainscoting and other handsome woodwork, as well as leaded art glass and 93 distinctive fireplaces. Gifford designed a majority of the other buildings.

Contemplating the ideal location for their hunting club, William K. Vanderbilt, J.P. Morgan, William Rockefeller, Joseph Pulitzer and 50 or so of their friends chose Jekyll Island. Its climate, abundant wildlife and natural beauty appealed to them. Once the decision was made, it took just two years to incorporate the club, purchase the island and have the clubhouse constructed.

In January of 1888, the men gathered their families and boarded their yachts for the first "season" on Jekyll. A collection of sepia photographs captures the spirit of these families as they enjoyed the island's outdoor pleasures ... hunting trips, lawn parties, carriage rides and leisurely afternoons at the beach. For years, there was unofficial competition among yachting members to see who would arrive in the longest, fastest, most beautifully appointed vessel.

Dinner each evening, however, was the high point of the day. Women spent hours selecting the dresses they would wear, while the men had definite ideas about what they hoped to accomplish during dinner conversations. Decisions might be made that would literally determine the next President, the health of the nation's economy or the career of any of their peers.

For example, when President McKinley was facing re-election, club member Cornelius Bliss was determined that "his man" would be successful. He and Marcus Hanna invited McKinley to Jekyll Island, and two days before he was to arrive, they learned Thomas B. Reed, Speaker of the House and McKinley's archrival, would be there at the same time. Bliss and Hanna arranged for the two men to meet, pressures were brought to bear and Reed ultimately did not oppose McKinley's re-election, even though he was adamantly opposed to the President's imperialistic policies regarding Cuba and the Philippines.

Finance was also of paramount concern to many club members. J.P. Morgan could create or quell panics on Wall Street with the financial resources at his personal command. Club members George Baker, head of the

First National Bank of New York, and James Stillman, head of the National City Bank of New York, were nearly as wealthy as Morgan. When an economic panic caused a run on the country's banks in 1907, one of these three men paved the way for a secret meeting on Jekyll. The purpose was to quickly and quietly develop a plan for a centralized banking structure, and the result was the creation of the plan for the Federal Reserve System.

Communications was the field of Theodore Vail, president of the company that later became AT&T. When his company laid the telephone lines in 1915 for the first transcontinental telephone call, he was convalescing on the island. He had the linemen lay the lines to Jekyll so he could participate in this momentous event in communications history.

World War I offered some club members the opportunity to give their yachts to the U.S. war effort and provide financial assistance. Although several of the men had had considerable influence in mitigating the force of economic panics throughout the last half of the 1800s and later, no one was powerful enough to prevent the Great Depression.

Just two years into the Depression, half the club's membership dropped away. The final blow was World War II and the threat of enemy submarines off the coast. Members left in 1942 expecting to return another year, but few ever did.

By 1947, the State of Georgia gained the ownership of the island and established it as a state park. Jekyll Development Associates leased the structures and grounds from the state, completely rejuvenated them and further prepared for the opening of Jekyll Island Club Hotel in 1986.

Guests today may choose from three restaurants—a dinner in the Grand Dining Room would celebrate the very spot where former members made those momentous decisions ... while the Courtyard at Crane and Café Solterra are worthy alternatives. Whether your primary interest is architecture or history, you will find a visit to Jekyll Island Club Hotel rewarding.

AVGOLEMONO
(GREEK EGG AND LEMON SOUP)

Serves 6

6 cups chicken broth
$1/3$ cup uncooked white rice
4 eggs, *separated*
Salt and white pepper to taste
Juice of 1 lemon

In a soup pot, bring broth to a simmer. Add rice and cook until tender, about 15 minutes. Whip egg yolks until thickened. Whip egg whites to soft peaks. Fold whites into the yolks; add to the simmering broth, whipping constantly. The soup will become frothy and thick. Season with salt, pepper and lemon juice.

FRIED GREEN TOMATOES
WITH SKORDALIA SAUCE

Serves 8

¹/₂ pound day-old bread, crusts removed

4 medium cloves garlic

1 teaspoon kosher salt

¹/₂ cup extra virgin olive oil

¹/₄ cup verjus (sour grape juice) *or* 2 tablespoons
   cider vinegar

Finely ground pepper to taste

¹/₃ cup warm water

2 pounds large firm green tomatoes (about 4)

¹/₂ cup all-purpose flour

Salt and pepper to taste

Pinch sugar

1¹/₂ cups vegetable oil

Salad greens

Tear bread into small pieces; soak in water until wet throughout. Press out excess water. With a mortar and pestle or on a smooth surface, crush garlic with kosher salt to purée. Put purée in a blender or food processor; add olive oil, verjus and pepper. While blending, slowly add warm water; blend until smooth. Set aside until serving.

Cut tomatoes into ⅜-inch-thick slices. Blend flour with salt, pepper and sugar. Heat vegetable oil in a large heavy skillet over medium-high heat. Dredge tomatoes in seasoned flour. Fry until lightly browned and crispy on both sides. Drain on paper towels. Season if desired.

To serve, arrange two or three tomato slices over salad greens; top with sauce.

BROILED LAMB CHOPS
WITH CREAMY MINT PESTO, CAPELLINI AND GORGONZOLA

Serves 6

¹/₄ cup pine nuts

3 large cloves garlic

1¹/₂ cups packed fresh mint leaves

¹/₄ teaspoon salt

¹/₈ teaspoon pepper

¹/₄ cup olive oil

1 tablespoon lemon juice

16 ounces capellini pasta

6 lamb loin chops

¹/₂ cup heavy whipping cream

³/₄ cup crumbled Gorgonzola

For pesto, in a food processor, combine the pine nuts, garlic, mint, salt and pepper; blend until smooth. Gradually add oil and lemon juice. Set aside.

Cook pasta according to package directions. Meanwhile, place lamb chops on a broiler pan. Broil 4 inches from the heat for 10 minutes, turning once, until light pink in center. In a saucepan, heat pesto and cream. Drain pasta; serve lamb chops over pasta with pesto sauce. Garnish with Gorgonzola, red flame grapes and fresh mint.

Wentworth Mansion

Wentworth Mansion®

149 Wentworth Street

Charleston, South Carolina

  29401

(843) 853-1886

(888) 466-1886

www.wentworthmansion.com

In 1881, wealthy cotton merchant Francis Silas Rodgers set out to build an elegant home in Charleston, South Carolina, worthy of his family of 13. Upon its completion in 1886, his vision was realized, and today the beautiful home is the luxurious 21-room Wentworth Mansion.

Rodgers hired only the finest of artisans. Daniel G. Waynes served as the architect for the nearly 14,000-square-foot, four-story home, creating the best example of Second Empire Style, characterized by its mansard roof, in Charleston. In fact, the home has been called the finest in Charleston, a city known for its architectural treasures.

While on a trip to Europe, Rodgers commissioned two magnificent matching chandeliers, which still hang today, and is said to have brought back their maker to ensure proper installation. A noted marble/stone worker and sculptor, Emile T. Viett, carved the elegant marble mantelpieces in the home's double parlors. Other features include Louis Comfort Tiffany glass panels, Philadelphia pressed brick and a rooftop cupola with panoramic views of the city.

Shortly after its completion, the home survived the great earthquake of August 1886, and records remain evidencing repairs of the damage. Rodgers and his heirs lived in the home until 1920, when it was sold to the Scottish Rite Cathedral Association, which sold it in 1940 to the Atlantic Coast Life Insurance Company.

Richard Widman, the current owner, purchased the house in 1997, recognizing that it had all the ingredients to become a fine luxury hotel. Amazingly, the building still retained many of its original architectural features, down to the custom-built louvered window treatments with the original Victorian hardware.

After a careful, 18-month restoration, Widman, architect Joe Schmidt, of Evans and Schmidt, and interior designer Pam Plowden, of Pulliam Morris Interiors in Columbia, South Carolina, transformed this once gracious home into an upscale hotel, blending elements of the past and present. They kept the original rooms intact while creatively designing other rooms to add a comfortable yet sumptuous décor.

In 2000, Widman converted the carriage house, which once housed the stables and carriages, into Circa 1886, recently acclaimed to be one of the most aesthetically pleasing restaurants in Charleston. Circa 1886 offers sophisticated Southern cuisine with a twist, and the menu changes seasonally to take advantage of the best ingredients of the region. Today, Wentworth Mansion® and Circa 1886 are part of the Charming Inns® family of six elegant and historical bed-and-breakfast inns.

SPICY SHRIMP

Serves 4–6

1 small shallot, peeled

2 cloves garlic, peeled

$^1/_4$ cup red hot sauce

$^3/_4$ cup canola oil

1 teaspoon salt

Pinch white pepper

2 pounds raw medium *or* large shrimp, peeled and deveined

Oil for frying

$^1/_2$ cup corn flour

$^1/_2$ cup all-purpose flour

2 tablespoons Old Bay Seasoning

1 green tomato, sliced $^1/_2$ inch thick

1 cup buttermilk

Place the shallot, garlic and hot sauce in a blender and blend until smooth. While blending, slowly add oil. Transfer to a shallow glass container; add salt, pepper and shrimp. Refrigerate for about 30 minutes.

In a fryer, heat oil to 350°. Mix the flours and Old Bay Seasoning; coat tomato slices with flour mixture, then dip in buttermilk and coat again with flour mixture. Fry until golden brown.

Remove shrimp from marinade and grill until pink, about 2 minutes each side. Serve over fried green tomato slices with a fresh tomato sauce.

CHOCOLATE GRAND MARNIER TRUFFLES

Makes 30 pieces

1/4 cup butter, cubed

5 tablespoons heavy whipping cream

7 ounces bittersweet chocolate, chopped

1 egg yolk

Grated peel of 1 orange

2 tablespoons Grand Marnier

Cocoa powder

In a small saucepan, combine butter and cream. Cook over low heat until the butter is melted and cream bubbles around the edges. Remove from the heat; add chocolate and stir until completely melted. Stir in the egg yolk, orange peel and Grand Marnier. Pour into a shallow container and chill.

Once chilled, scoop and form into bite-size balls; roll in sifted cocoa powder. Serve chilled.

THE SOUTHWEST

Arizona, New Mexico, Oklahoma and Texas. The attraction of the Southwest is best embodied in visits to places like the Alamo, a ranch that would be the envy of cattle barons throughout the world (King Ranch), the National Cowboy Hall of Fame, Carlsbad Caverns National Park, Gila Cliff Dwellings National Monument, Tombstone (site of the famous shootout at the OK Corral) or the Grand Canyon. Numerous large cities offer rest and great restaurants, both a reflection of the region's warmth and hospitality.

The Atherton Hotel at OSU

The Union Club Hotel opened September 10, 1950 as the premier location for overnight visitors to the Oklahoma State University campus. From the start, it was more than just a place to stay on campus. Comfort and convenience were paramount considerations, and this philosophy is still evident today.

Among the special features in the original 82 guestrooms were eye-appealing furnishings, wall-to-wall carpeting, air-conditioning, private bath and telephone service. The hotel became known for having circulating ice water—a faucet with chilled water in the system. The Union Club had automatic elevator service and ample parking space adjacent to the entrances. Moderate room rates appealed to parents and university guests.

Renovations in 1986 included new Georgian furniture, carpeting and drapes. In 2001, it was renamed the Atherton Hotel at OSU in honor of Bill Atherton, an OSU graduate who spearheaded the renovation.

The Atherton is now part of the university's College of Human Environmental Sciences and the School of Hotel and Restaurant Administration, serving as a "living laboratory" for future professionals in the hospitality business. Only four other such facilities exist on college campuses across the USA.

Famous hotel guests have included Presidents Truman, Ford, Carter, Reagan and Bush, Bob Hope, Haile Selassie, Vincent Price, Wilt Chamberlain, Will Rogers Jr., Suzanne Sommers, Bill Crosby, Faith Hill, Sinbad, and Senators John Edwards and Joseph Lieberman.

A recent $6 million renovation has given the hotel a stately elegance and sophistication in a warm and inviting atmosphere. The Atherton is dedicated to offering hospitality with quality, style and sophistication founded in a rich heritage and tradition. By providing students with the opportunity to be a part of this unique learning experience, the Atherton is creating a legacy of distinction.

The Atherton Hotel at OSU

H103 Student Union

Stillwater, Oklahoma 74078

(405) 744-6835

www.athertonhotelatosu.com

PISTOL PETE PECAN BALL

Serves 1

1 cup vanilla ice cream
½ cup chopped pecans
Chocolate sauce
Caramel ice cream topping

Form the ice cream into a round ball. Roll in pecans until well coated. Place on a plate drizzled with chocolate sauce and caramel topping. Garnish with fresh fruit and cream.

"Pistol Pete" has been the mascot of the Oklahoma State University Cowboys since 1923.

STRAWBERRIES WITH CREAM

Serves 8-10

4 teaspoons unflavored gelatin
$1/4$ cup cold water
2 cups half-and-half cream
$1/4$ cup sugar
2 cups sour cream
1 pint fresh strawberries, cored and sliced*
$1/2$ pint heavy whipping cream, whipped

Soften the gelatin in cold water. In a saucepan, scald the half-and-half and sugar. Remove from the heat; add gelatin and stir until dissolved. Transfer to a bowl. Chill until thickened. Fold in the sour cream and blend until smooth. Turn into an oiled 1-quart mold. Chill until firm. Unmold dessert. Serve with strawberries and whipped cream.

*Strawberries can be mixed in with the cream mixture and poured into the mold instead of serving on top.

MERINGUE ROULADE

Serves 16

10 egg whites
1 teaspoon vinegar
1 pound castor (superfine) sugar
2 tablespoons confectioners' sugar
2 teaspoons cornstarch
2 cups heavy whipping cream
1 cup lemon curd

Line two half sheet pans with parchment paper. In a mixing bowl, beat the egg whites and vinegar on high until stiff peaks form. Reduce the speed. Combine the sugars and cornstarch; gradually add to egg white mixture and beat for 30 seconds. Evenly divide mixture between the prepared pans, spreading out evenly into all corners. Bake at 300° for 35 minutes. Cool.

Lightly dust a second piece of parchment paper with confectioners' sugar. Turn out one of the meringues onto the dusted parchment and remove the parchment it was baked on. Whip cream to soft peaks. Spread an even layer of lemon curd over meringue; top with a layer of whipped cream. Gently roll up the meringue, using the parchment if needed as a guide. Using an electric knife, cut into 1-inch slices. Serve with fresh fruit and cream.

The Driskill Hotel

The Driskill Hotel

604 Brazos Street

Austin, Texas 78701

(512) 474-5911

www.driskillhotel.com

Cattle baron Jesse Lincoln Driskill built his hotel in 1886 to serve as the South's Frontier Palace. His attention to detail and desire to create an architectural masterpiece made Texans justifiably proud. He spent $400,000, an enormous sum of money for the time.

A special edition of the *Austin Daily Statesman* described the hotel as "one of the finest in the country" and went on to say that it was "a blessing to the city and state, which cannot be overestimated."

Less than two weeks after the grand opening, the hotel hosted the first inaugural ball for Texas Governor Sul Ross. With a tradition established, later governors William Hobby, Dan Moody and John Connally also used the Driskill for their inauguration celebrations.

In 1887, Colonel Driskill's livelihood was threatened by a nationwide drought. The following year, an exceptionally cold winter wiped out 3,000 head of his cattle, and he was forced to sell his beloved hotel. A series of owners followed, as well as renovations and improvements that included the first long-distance telephone service in the city.

With its stained-glass dome, fine antiques, oil paintings, massive draperies and inlaid marble floors, the hotel seems more like a stately grand estate ... while the leather sofas, plush carpets and Texas accoutrements give it the feel of a private club.

Every guestroom is unique in its décor. There are 188 rooms and suites in two wings—the Historic Wing, which features soaring ceilings and elaborate woodwork, and the Traditional Wing, which was built in 1929 and is decorated in the colors of the Texas Hill Country.

Renowned for its traditional fare, regional sensations and ever-changing novel creations, the Driskill Grill is a majestic setting for any celebration. The restaurant has been the recipient of *Wine Spectator's* Award of Excellence and AAA's Four Diamond Award, among others.

In 1934, Texas natives Lyndon and Lady Bird Johnson had their first date at the hotel—breakfast in the dining room. Thus began the couple's lifelong "love affair" with the hotel. The Governor's Suite on the fifth floor was permanently reserved for LBJ, who awaited his election results at the hotel when he ran for Vice President in 1960.

Over the years, the Driskill has hosted many other famous guests, including Amelia Earhart, Louis Armstrong, Michael Jordan, Paul Simon, Sandra Bullock, President and Mrs. Clinton, and President and Mrs. Bush. But you needn't be a celebrity to receive a Texas-sized welcome at the historic Driskill ... y'all come visit!

PROSCIUTTO-WRAPPED SEA SCALLOPS
WITH CUCUMBER TOMATO SALAD

Serves 4

12 sea scallops, muscle removed

12 paper-thin slices prosciutto

Salt to taste

Creamy Vinaigrette

$1/2$ cup sour cream

$1/4$ cup mayonnaise

$1/4$ cup white wine

1 teaspoon white truffle oil

1 teaspoon capers

Salt and lemon juice to taste

Cucumber Tomato Salad

$1/2$ English cucumber

2 large red heirloom tomatoes, julienned

2 large yellow heirloom tomatoes, julienned

$1/2$ small red onion, julienned

1 teaspoon finely chopped fresh dill

Wrap each scallop with prosciutto. Season with salt. In an ovenproof skillet, sauté scallops over high heat for 1–2 minutes on each side or until golden brown. Finish in a 350° oven for 3–5 minutes.

For vinaigrette, combine the sour cream, mayonnaise, wine, oil and capers in a blender; purée until smooth. Season with salt and lemon juice.

Cut the cucumber in half lengthwise and remove the seeds; cut cucumber into half-moon shapes. In a bowl, combine the cucumber, tomatoes, onion and dill; toss with ¾ cup vinaigrette.

To serve, divide the cucumber tomato salad among four plates. Place three scallops around the salad on each plate; drizzle remaining vinaigrette around the scallops.

JALAPEÑO MASHED POTATOES
WITH SWEET CORN SAUCE

Serves 6

3 Idaho potatoes, peeled and cubed

Salt

¹/₄ cup heavy whipping cream

6 tablespoons salted butter

3 jalapeños, roasted, skin and seeds removed, diced

Sweet Corn Sauce

2 tablespoons canola oil

1 shallot, chopped

¹/₄ teaspoon ground cumin

3 ears of corn, shucked and kernels removed

2 cups chicken stock

Lime juice, maple syrup and salt to taste

Place the potatoes in a large saucepan and cover with water; add salt. Bring to a boil. Reduce heat to medium; cook until fork-tender. Meanwhile, in a small saucepan over medium heat, bring the cream and butter to a boil.

Drain the potatoes; press through a food mill or whip until incorporated. Add cream mixture as needed to obtain desired consistency. Add the jalapeños and season with salt. Keep warm.

For sauce, heat oil in a small saucepan over medium heat; sauté shallot for 1 minute. Add cumin and toast for 1 minute. Add the corn and cook for 1 minute. Stir in the stock; bring to a boil and cook for 5 minutes. Purée in a blender until smooth. Strain through a fine mesh sieve. Season with lime juice, syrup and salt. Serve with mashed potatoes.

Hotel Galvez

Hotel Galvez

2024 Seawall Boulevard

Galveston, Texas 77550

(409) 765-7721

www.wyndham.com

After the Great Storm of 1900—when a massive hurricane devastated Galveston, Texas—a group of prominent businessmen, dedicated to the economic recovery of the island, knew there was a desperate need of a luxury beachfront hotel to fill the void that was left when the Beach Hotel burned down in 1898.

At a cost of more than $1 million, the St. Louis firm of Mauran & Russell designed and built Hotel Galvez—a six-story Spanish Colonial Revival building named for Bernardo de Galvez, the Spanish colonial governor who chartered the Texas Gulf Coast and for whom the city is named. When it opened in 1911, the luxury hotel offered 275 elegant guestrooms, some with private baths. In 1912, *Hotel Monthly* billed it as one of the "most richly furnished seaside hotels in America."

The public areas featured a barbershop, candy shop, drugstore, soda fountain and Gentleman's Bar & Grille. Roller chairs lined the front of the hotel for those wanting to take a trip along the famed Seawall Boulevard.

In 1918, Hotel Galvez hosted more than 400 guests each day, with room rates starting at $2 per night. In the 1920s, the first bathing beauty contests in the nation were held at the hotel, with future movie stars Joan Blondell and Dorothy Lamour as participants.

During the '20s and '30s, Hotel Galvez became known as the "Playground of the Southwest," as hundreds of celebrities and dignitaries stayed there. Notable guests included Presidents Franklin Roosevelt, Dwight Eisenhower, Lyndon Johnson and John Kennedy, as well as General Douglas MacArthur, Phil Harris, Alice Faye, Frank Sinatra, Jimmy Stewart and Howard Hughes.

On October 3, 1940, W.L. Moody Jr. acquired Hotel Galvez. During World War II, the hotel served as a living and working facility for the U.S. Coast Guard. In 1950, Moody's hotel chain, National Affiliated Hotels, added a motel on the east side of the main building.

In 1965, the owners spent more than $1 million to refurbish the hotel. Another million-dollar-plus renovation was undertaken by the next owners, Harvey O. McCarthy and Dr. Leon Bromberg, who acquired the hotel in 1971.

Hotel Galvez changed hands again in 1978, when it was purchased by well-known heart surgeon Denton Cooley, who had a long-standing sentimental attachment to it. Not only had he stayed there as a child and medical student, but his parents spent their wedding night at the hotel in 1916. Cooley sold half of his interest to Archie Bennett Jr., president of the Mariner Corporation.

In 1980, the partners spent one year and more than $12 million renovating the hotel, after which it was named to the National Register of Historic Places.

The most recent renovation was brought about through the efforts of Galveston preservationists and developers George and Cynthia Mitchell, who attained

ownership of Hotel Galvez in March of 1993. Since June 1, 1998, Wyndham International as Wyndham Historic Hotels has managed the hotel.

Today, Hotel Galvez stands proudly as "Queen of the Gulf," fully restored to its original glamour while continuing to offer gracious hospitality, old-world charm and new-world conveniences.

Towering palms and lushly landscaped grounds surround a restored grand seawall entrance. Guests can relax around the tropical pool, which features a swim-up bar. The menu at Bernardo's, the hotel's restaurant, offers a wide variety of choices. The newly renovated 224 guestrooms and seven suites offer ocean vistas and panoramic views of historic Galveston.

GRILLED ASPARAGUS
WITH GAZPACHO VINAIGRETTE

Serves 1

Gazpacho Vinaigrette

1 cucumber, peeled and seeded

6 Roma tomatoes, peeled

3 shallots

Juice of 4 lemons

1 cup tomato juice

2 tablespoons chopped flat leaf parsley

2 cloves garlic

$^1/_2$ cup chopped green onion tops

Salt and freshly ground black pepper to taste

$^1/_2$ tablespoon Tabasco

Additional lemon juice

Extra virgin oil olive

Eggplant Croutons

$^1/_2$ cup cubed peeled eggplant

$^1/_4$ cup milk

$^1/_4$ cup semolina

Oil for frying

Salt to taste

Salad

$^1/_2$ pound asparagus spears

1 teaspoon extra virgin olive oil

Kosher salt and freshly ground black pepper to taste

1 tablespoon diced cucumber

1 tablespoon diced seeded tomato

1 teaspoon finely diced celery

1 teaspoon finely diced red onion

$^1/_2$ teaspoon minced flat leaf parsley

Cut cucumber into pieces and place in a food processor or blender; add tomatoes, shallots, lemon juice, tomato juice, parsley, garlic and green onion tops. Pulse to purée. Transfer to a bowl; season with Tabasco, salt and pepper.

To finish the vinaigrette, for each cup of gazpacho, add the juice of one lemon and 1 cup extra virgin olive oil; blend using a hand blender until thickened and frothy.

For the croutons, dip cubed eggplant in milk, then dredge in semolina. In a deep fryer, heat oil to 375°; fry eggplant until lightly browned. Drain on paper towel. Season immediately with salt.

Trim, peel and blanch the asparagus; toss with oil. Season with salt and pepper. Place in the center of the plate. Ladle 3 tablespoons gazpacho vinaigrette over the asparagus. Garnish with cucumber, tomato, celery, red onion, parsley and eggplant croutons.

MEYER LEMON TART

Crust

$1/3$ cup plus $1/4$ cup unsalted butter,
   room temperature, cubed

$1/2$ cup confectioners' sugar, sifted

1 egg

2 cups all-purpose flour

$1/8$ teaspoon baking powder

Filling

4 Meyer lemons

4 eggs

$1\,1/4$ cups sugar

$1/3$ cup unsalted butter, melted

In a mixing bowl, beat butter and confectioners' sugar on low speed until smooth, about 3 minutes. Add egg and beat until creamy. Using a rubber spatula, fold in the flour and baking powder just until incorporated. Beat on low until dough is evenly mixed and clings together, 2–3 minutes. Shape into a ball; wrap tightly in plastic wrap and refrigerate for at least 2 hours.

Bring dough to room temperature. Brush the bottom and sides of a 9-inch tart pan with melted butter. On a lightly floured surface, roll dough into a 12-inch circle about $1/8$ inch thick. Drape dough over a rolling pin and transfer to prepared tart pan; unwrap dough from pin and press it gently into pan. Roll pin over the top of the pan to remove excess dough. Place waxed paper over pastry and add pie weights. Bake at 400° until the pastry is half cooked, about 15 minutes.

Meanwhile, for filling, grate the zest from the lemons and reserve; cut lemons in half and squeeze the juice through a strainer into a measuring cup. (You should have about ½ cup of juice.) In a large bowl, whisk the lemon juice, eggs and lemon zest until blended. Add sugar and mix until well combined. Stir in melted butter.

Remove tart shell from the oven and immediately remove the weights and waxed paper. Pour filling into shell. Bake until the filling is set and the edges are golden brown, about 20 minutes. Place on a wire rack. Remove sides of pan; cool completely. Serve at room temperature.

The Hermosa Inn

The Hermosa Inn

5532 North Palo Cristi Road

Paradise Valley, Arizona

  85253

(602) 955-8614

(800) 241-1210

www.hermosainn.com

When cowboy artist Alonzo "Lon" Megargee set his eyes on an isolated plot of land in Arizona's Paradise Valley, it spoke to him. He built a one-room studio in the middle of it and called it home. Bordered by Squaw Peak to the north, the canal to the south, Camelback Mountain to the east and the wide-open desert to the west, Paradise Valley was far beyond the Phoenix city limits in the 1930s.

A Philadelphia native, Megargee came West at the turn of the century, chasing the American dream and earning his way as a cowboy, broncobuster, stud poker dealer, commercial artist and home builder. His charm snared several wives and earned him a reputation as a ladies' man. But it was his adobe studio that perhaps was the closest to his heart.

Functioning without formal plans but influenced by the architecture he'd studied in Mexico and Spain, Megargee used adobe blocks mixed and formed on site with the sandy desert soil, and he found old beams and wood from an abandoned mine. He aged the exterior walls by pouring a mixture of oil and ash over them from the roof. It took him several years, but Megargee created a uniquely Southwestern home he dubbed "Casa Hermosa"—Beautiful House.

To supplement his art income, Megargee began running Casa Hermosa as a guest ranch. A bachelor at the time, he was already hosting many of his friends who came to stay for extended visits, so it seemed natural. Most of his business was legal, although the sheriff did make several unannounced visits to check on rumors of late-night gambling sessions. Megargee thoughtfully provided guests with secret tunnels from the main house to the stables so they could disappear into the desert if needed.

By 1941, in the midst of a divorce and in need of money, Mcgargee put Casa Hermosa, filled with his art and furnishings, on the market. The new owners, who had every intention of using the property as their private home, were surprised late one night by a taxi-full of guests and found themselves in the guest ranch business.

Succeeding owners added a pool, tennis courts and the Casitas and Villas, and the name was changed to the Hermosa Resort. It became the center of social life for the neighbors, who swam in the pool and used it as an extra bedroom for their guests.

In the late 1980s, Hermosa Resort was caught in the real estate and savings-and-loan crisis that touched most of the West. In addition, a devastating fire in 1987 severely damaged the main building, Megargee's old home.

Paradise Valley residents Fred and Jennifer Unger, who were intrigued with the resort and its history, bought the property in 1992 and set out to restore its charm. The Ungers worked with builder and designer Dan MacBeth, also a Paradise Valley resident, to save the adobe walls of the fire-damaged building, restore the charred old beams and clean up the original ironwork that graces the building inside and out.

The interior of the building, which now houses the reception area and LON's *at the hermosa* restaurant, was furnished to reflect a 1930s Southwestern ambience, much like it was during Megargee's days. Prints and originals of his artwork and photographs of him hang on the walls.

LON's *at the hermosa* is the only remaining authentic hacienda in Arizona. Guests can enjoy award-winning American cuisine, wood-grilled steaks, fresh seafood and an extensive wine list in the adobe dining room or outdoors on the patio.

The Hermosa Inn's seclusion and privacy attract guests seeking high-level corporate retreats as well as those looking for a serene desert oasis. The courtyard features fountains and fireplaces, and pathways ramble through the 6½-acre grounds, marked by olive and mesquite trees, towering palms, fragrant citrus trees and brilliant flowers.

The inn is conveniently located 10 minutes from the Phoenix airport and all major highways in and around Phoenix and Scottsdale, so those cities' best events and attractions are just moments away.

LAMB AT THE HERMOSA

Serves 1

4 to 6 tablespoons extra virgin olive oil, *divided*

2 to 3 tablespoons lemon juice

2 teaspoons chopped fresh marjoram

$1/2$ teaspoon minced garlic

$1/4$ teaspoon pepper

7 ounces lamb loin *or* rib chops

Additional oil

6 asparagus spears, trimmed

$1/4$ cup grape *or* pear tomatoes (or other tiny tomatoes), halved

1 to 2 tablespoons balsamic vinegar

1 large vine-ripe tomato, sliced

Coarse salt and freshly ground black pepper

In a shallow glass container, combine 2–3 tablespoons oil, lemon juice, marjoram, garlic and pepper. Add lamb chops and refrigerate for several hours. Drain and discard marinade. Lightly oil the lamb and season with salt. Grill until meat reaches desired doneness.

Oil the asparagus and season with salt and pepper; grill. Dress the tiny tomatoes with vinegar and remaining oil. Shingle the tomato slices on a serving plate; place lamb chops on plate. Arrange asparagus and a mound of tiny tomatoes alongside. Sprinkle with coarse salt and apply a few twists of the pepper mill.

ORANGE AND JICAMA WITH CHAYOTE

Serves 1

3 orange slices ($1/2$ inch thick)

3 medium leaves butter lettuce

1 to 2 tablespoons diced jicama

1 to 2 tablespoons diced chayote (mirliton)

$1/2$ teaspoon pickled julienned carrot

$1/2$ lime

Dash cayenne pepper

Hazelnut oil

Micro greens

Place the orange slices on a chilled salad plate. Lay lettuce leaves over oranges, but don't cover completely. Toss the jicama and chayote and place over lettuce. Top with pickled carrot. Squeeze the lime over the salad and sprinkle with cayenne. Drizzle with hazelnut oil and garnish with micro greens.

La Fonda

La Fonda

100 East San Francisco Street

Santa Fe, New Mexico 87501

(505) 982-5511

(800) 523-5002

www.lafondasantafe.com

When visiting America's oldest capital city, it's only appropriate to stay at historic lodging ... so La Fonda is the ideal choice for a stay in Santa Fe, New Mexico. The landmark structure, recognized by the National Trust for Historic Preservation, has long been at the heart of the city.

An inn (fonda) was among the first businesses established when Santa Fe was founded in 1607. More than 200 years later, when Captain William Becknell completed the first successful trading expedition from Missouri to Santa Fe in 1821, he enjoyed the hospitality at the inn on the town's central plaza. Becknell's route, which ended at the plaza, came to be known as the Santa Fe Trail.

The current La Fonda was built in 1922 on the historic plaza, on the site of the previous inns. In 1925, it was acquired by the Atchison, Topeka & Santa Fe Railroad, which leased it to Fred Harvey. For more than 40 years, from 1926 to 1968, La Fonda was one of the Harvey Houses, a renowned chain of fine hotels.

Since 1968, La Fonda has been locally owned and operated and has continued the tradition of providing warm hospitality and excellent service. The integrity of the authentic pueblo-style architecture and décor has been maintained while modern amenities have been added.

Today, the hotel features 167 guestrooms and suites, plus 14 luxury accommodations in its La Terraza rooftop retreat. There is an outdoor pool and hot tub, exercise facilities and Internet access throughout. At the charming La Plazuela restaurant, guests can enjoy guacamole made tableside and other dishes prepared with fresh, locally grown ingredients.

Santa Fe has long been known for its fine art galleries, and La Fonda displays the work of local artisans. It even has a staff artist, Ernest Martinez, who has been working at the hotel for over 50 years, painting murals, furniture, tiles and more ... adding those little details that give the place its Southwestern ambience.

The city is also the home of the Georgia O'Keeffe Museum, telling the story of the artist who made her home in Santa Fe and displaying her beautiful paintings. Plus there are countless must-see sites in the surrounding area, such as the Taos ski valley and Los Alamos, site of the National Laboratory. Use La Fonda as a home base for a vacation in the Land of Enchantment.

FRIJOLES CHARROS

Serves 32

¹/₂ pound yellow onions, diced

2 ounces lard

¹/₂ pound bacon, cut into 1-inch pieces

¹/₂ pound fully cooked ham, cubed

6 ounces chorizo

1¹/₂ teaspoons minced garlic

¹/₂ pound tomatoes, diced

5 serrano chiles, sliced

1 gallon pinto beans, cooked

1¹/₄ ounces pork chicharrón

¹/₂ bunch cilantro, chopped

Salt and pepper to taste

In a large pot, sauté onions in lard until translucent. Add bacon, ham, chorizo and garlic. When bacon is fully cooked, stir in the tomatoes and chiles. Add the cooked beans, chicharrón, cilantro, salt and pepper. Simmer until heated through and flavors are blended.

DRIED CHERRY-MANGO CHUTNEY

2 pounds dried cherries
1/2 pound red onions, diced
2 to 3 teaspoons minced garlic
1/2 cup packed brown sugar
2 pounds fresh mangoes, peeled and diced
3/4 cup cider vinegar
Pinch cinnamon, allspice and ground cloves
Salt and pepper to taste

Place the cherries in a bowl and cover with boiling water; steep until water is absorbed. In a large saucepan, sweat onions and garlic. Add brown sugar; cook for 2 minutes. Add cherries, mangoes, vinegar, spices, salt and pepper. Simmer until reduced to desired consistency.

BUTTERNUT SQUASH SOUP

Serves 8–10
1/2 ounce fresh gingerroot, minced
1 cup white wine
1/4 pound onions, diced
1/4 pound celery, diced
1 to 1 1/2 teaspoons minced garlic
2 tablespoons vegetable oil
2 1/2 pounds butternut squash, cooked
1/2 cup vegetable stock
1 cup heavy whipping cream
Salt and pepper to taste

Steep the ginger in wine. In a large saucepan or soup pot, sweat the onions, celery and garlic in oil. Add the cooked squash, stock and ginger-wine mixture; bring to a boil. Cool slightly; purée in a blender. Return to the pan; heat through. Heat the cream; stir into soup. Season with salt and pepper.

THE MOUNTAIN PLAINS

Colorado, Idaho, Kansas, Nebraska, North Dakota, Montana, South Dakota, Utah and Wyoming. The rolling high-country plains and mountains of this region emphasize the wide-open spaces between the three coasts of the U.S. Spring-fed rivers, snow-covered ski slopes and dude ranches are all part of this magnificent area, which draws visitors from throughout the world. Dining is a great attraction, especially in the popular tourist destinations and historic towns in Colorado.

The Brown Palace Hotel

The Brown Palace Hotel

321 17th Street

Denver, Colorado 80202

(303) 297-3111

(800) 321-2599

www.brownpalace.com

The red granite and sandstone walls of the Brown Palace Hotel have watched more than a century of Colorado history develop. Denver was a mere 34 years old when Henry C. Brown opened the doors of his monument to himself in August 1892.

It was a braggart city built by men who'd made fortunes on the gold and silver drawn from the same mountains they viewed from their mansions on Capitol Hill, where Brown had first homesteaded. They welcomed the new, elegant locale in which to conduct their business deals. Their wives took tea and their daughters danced at lavish balls.

It was fittingly a palace for "The Queen City of the Plains," as Denver dubbed itself. Inside the hotel, designed by architect Frank E. Edbrooke, the eight-story atrium rivaled the grandest of hotels "back East," with its pillars and wainscoting of pale golden onyx from Mexico reflecting the pastel shades of the stained-glass ceiling. A massive fireplace, the mantel of which was supported by two solid pillars of onyx, was a welcome amenity when the winter winds howled down from the snowcapped peaks.

Through the years, the Brown Palace has seen it all—boom times and depressions, peace and war. Emperors and presidents, kings and queens, and stars of stage and screen have been closeted here. We can only imagine some of the stories. Others we know.

Teddy Roosevelt was the first President to stop at the Brown Palace Hotel. He came to Colorado to hunt bear in the spring of 1905. He spoke to businessmen, who only paid $10 to attend.

President and Mrs. Dwight Eisenhower were the most frequent First Family visitors to the Brown Palace. It served as Ike's pre-campaign headquarters in 1952, and they spent many summer vacations here. In 1955, the President had a travel allowance of $40,000 per year. A reporter estimated that an eight-week vacation in Denver would cost $25,000, including lodging and meals for his staff and Secret Service agents.

To commemorate their visits, the former Presidential Suite was renamed the Eisenhower Suite in 1980. A wayward golf ball Ike hit while practicing in the room made the dent in the fireplace mantel ... it remains today. Eisenhower stories are recounted during the twice-weekly historical tours.

During President Harding's stay in July 1923, a report said, "The White House for a few hours is on the eighth floor of the Brown Palace Hotel, and it will hold this temporary site until the party resumes its western jaunt at 1:30 this afternoon."

In the 1890s, a German count who had been banned from home over a small indiscretion ran out of funds while living it up in the United States. He worked as a bookkeeper at the Brown Palace for over a year. In 1903, Count D'Agreneff, a Russian nobleman, worked as a barber at the hotel and shaved President McKinley when he visited Denver. Another royal employee was Baron Gottfried von Kroenberger, a

WWI ace for Germany who flew with von Richthofen. He was headwaiter when the hotel opened the Palace Arms in 1950.

Sun Yat-sen, just prior to being appointed the first President of the New Republic of China in 1911, was in Denver raising money to free his countrymen from the Manchu Dynasty. While he was staying at the Brown Palace, the Revolution broke out and a Republic was proclaimed.

When Queen Marie of Romania visited Denver in 1926, she attended many royal functions, including a banquet at the Brown Palace Hotel. One of the reasons for her visit was to raise money to bolster her country's sickly finances. It is not surprising, then, that she spent an hour at the Denver Dry Goods store endorsing a new line of vacuum cleaners.

More than 700 wrought-iron grillwork panels ring the lobby from the third through the seventh floors. Two of them are upside down, one to serve the tradition that man, who cannot be perfect, must put a flaw into his handiwork; the other was sneaked in by a disgruntled workman. Finding these bits of history intrigue visitors to the Brown Palace Hotel.

CRÊPES SUZETTE

Serves 4

6 eggs

1 quart whole milk

4 cups all-purpose flour

$^1/_2$ cup sugar

Zest of 2 oranges, finely minced

2 tablespoons butter, melted

Sauce

1 tablespoon butter

2 tablespoons sugar

1 orange, halved and wrapped in cheesecloth

$^1/_2$ lemon, wrapped in cheesecloth

1 tablespoon Cointreau

2 tablespoons Grand Marnier

For crêpe batter, combine the eggs, milk, flour, sugar and orange zest in a bowl; mix well. Strain through a fine mesh sieve; refrigerate overnight.

Stir in melted butter. Mixture should coat the back of a spoon; thin with milk if necessary to achieve that consistency. Heat a nonstick sauté pan; coat evenly with batter and cook over medium heat until lightly brown. Turn over and briefly finish. Set aside. Continue to make crêpes one at a time.

For sauce, melt butter in a pan over medium heat. Add sugar and cook for 30 seconds. Squeeze orange and lemon over pan to completely juice them. Add Cointreau. Cook mixture to a syrupy consistency, about 1 minute. Add crêpes and turn over once. Carefully add Grand Marnier and flambé.

Remove crêpes to serving plates. Scoop chocolate and/or vanilla ice cream over crêpes. Spoon leftover syrup on top. Garnish with mint chiffonade, kumquat halves and orange zest if desired.

BEEF WELLINGTON

Serves 10

4 pounds beef tenderloin

1 teaspoon salt

Pepper to taste

2 cups finely chopped mushrooms

2 cups finely chopped shallots

1 tablespoon butter

White wine

4 to 6 ounces foie gras paté

2 tablespoons diced truffles, optional

1 puff pastry sheet

2 pieces sandwich bread, toasted

2 eggs, beaten

2 envelopes Madeira sauce

Season tenderloin with salt and pepper; sear and cool. For duxelles, in a skillet, sauté the mushrooms and shallots in butter. Season with salt and pepper. Add enough wine to moisten; mixture should be moist enough to hold together, but not runny.

Combine duxelles, foie gras and truffles if desired. Spread evenly over one side of tenderloin. Roll out pastry to $\frac{3}{16}$-inch thickness. Place tenderloin in center of pastry, with duxelle side down. Spread remaining duxelle mixture over top of tenderloin.

Trim toasted bread to fit on top of tenderloin and place over meat. Fold pastry over top; brush with egg wash. Turn over so meat is now sitting on top of toasted bread.

Trim sides of pastry and fold underneath; seal seams with egg wash. Decorate with pastry scraps as desired. Place on a baking sheet. Bake at 350° for 40–45 minutes (dough should be cooked through and golden brown; meat should have an internal temperature of 115°). While it's baking, prepare Madeira sauce according to package directions. Cut Wellington into ¾-inch slices; serve with sauce.

"To eat is a necessity; to eat intelligently is an art."
–Francois La Rochefoucauld

The Cliff House at Pikes Peak

The Cliff House at Pikes Peak

306 Cañon Avenue

Manitou Springs, Colorado
   80829

(719) 685-3000

(888) 212-7000

www.thecliffhouse.com

Travelers once just passed through Manitou Springs, never staying for long. It was a stagecoach stop on the route from Colorado Springs to Leadville, one of the most famous stagecoach runs in the American West. Manitou Springs grew up around the gold mines in the Pikes Peak area in the late 1850s, and when those mines proved bountiful, that all changed.

The building that had been the stagecoach stop was converted into a 20-room boardinghouse known simply as "The Inn." The earliest guests were mostly trappers and hunters on their way to or from Colorado Springs. But soon gold seekers made their way through Manitou Springs, bringing more business to the small inn. On occasion, tents had to be pitched next to the building to accommodate the overflow of guests.

By 1876, when the gold strikes were fewer and far between, the inn was struggling. That's when a mineral of another sort—mineral springs—came to play a role in the inn's fortunes.

Manitou Springs was home to ancient mineral springs, which bubbled up from underground limestone aquifers and carbonated the water—it was cool, good-tasting and had a high concentration of beneficial minerals. American Indians had been drinking it straight from the springs, believing them to have healing powers.

It was also in the 1870s that a man named Edward E. Nichols came west to fight a battle with tuberculosis. Nichols moved permanently to Manitou Springs,

where he served as mayor for eight terms. He bought the inn in 1886, renamed it the Cliff House and turned it into a sophisticated hotel that capitalized on the region's springs and sparkling waters.

In 1914, Nichols and Colorado Governor Oliver Shoup founded the Manitou Bath House Company. The entire community became a resort specializing in water therapies, and people were eager to visit and take advantage of the healing powers of the springs. In the 30 years that followed, Nichols expanded the hotel from 20 rooms to 56, and eventually to 200. The result was the beautiful, four-and-a-half-story building that still stands today.

The Cliff House had evolved into a desirable destination in its own right, attracting a well-heeled clientele, including Theodore Roosevelt; Ferdinand, Crown Prince of Austria; William Henry Jackson; Charles Dickens Jr.; P.T. Barnum; Thomas Edison; Clark Gable; F.W. Woolworth; and J. Paul Getty.

Each morning, guests were given programs detailing the evening's entertainment. They enjoyed a formal dinner, then delighted in a concert on the hotel grounds. Afterward, they were encouraged to walk across the street to Soda Springs for a glass of fresh springwater before retiring. The Cliff House even had underground tunnels leading from the hotel to the spa.

In later years, a bathhouse was built at the spa, and bellboys from the hotel would cross to the spring to fill bottles and glasses with sparkling water for the guests. The Cliff House at Pikes Peak soon became the most popular hotel and spa in the Colorado Springs region, drawing people from all walks of life and from around the world.

For all its successes, the Cliff House also endured some hard times. In 1921, a flash flood roared down Williams Canyon and washed through the hotel's Grill Room, a small sandwich and soda shop in the rear of the East wing, buckling the floor all the way to the ceiling.

California real estate developer James S. Morley bought the Cliff House in 1981, converting the historic building into a 42-unit apartment building. But in its second disaster of the century, the building caught fire in March 1982. The fourth-floor roof sustained so much damage it had to be replaced, and the interior was stripped of all plumbing, plaster and floor coverings. The water damage was so extensive that the entire building was threatened. Immediate action was taken to preserve what remained. Due to the local economy, the building stood vacant for 16 years.

Since the Cliff House had been placed on the National Register of Historic Places, the fire also raised concerns among citizens groups and government agencies that supported its renovation.

In 1997, Morley committed to the restoration, vowing to return the hotel to its original distinction, preserving the Rocky Mountain Victorian architecture of the 1800s, but incorporating 21st century state-of-the-art technology and amenities. After $9 million worth of refurbishing and loving care, this vision has been realized.

SWEET CORN BISQUE

Serves 8-10

2 medium yellow onions, finely diced
2 leeks (white portion only), finely diced
1/4 pound butter
4 cups sweet corn kernels
1/2 cup all-purpose flour
3 cups chicken stock
1 1/2 cups heavy whipping cream
Salt and pepper to taste

In a large saucepan or soup pot over high heat, sauté onions and leeks in butter until soft with just a little color. Reduce heat to medium. Add corn; cook for 10–15 minutes. Stir in flour (this will thicken the mixture almost like a paste). Continue to cook for about 5 minutes. Add stock. Bring to a boil; reduce heat and simmer for 15–20 minutes.

Remove from the heat. Using a hand blender, purée the soup until smooth. While blending, slowly add cream. Return to the heat; bring to a simmer. Run the soup through a fine mesh strainer. Season with salt and pepper. Garnish as desired; this soup is great with lobster, smoked chicken, grilled squash and any aromatic herbs.

DUCK A L'ORANGE

Serves 8

Frangelico Bread Pudding

1 pound bread, cut into thin slices

2 tablespoons unsalted butter, melted

8 eggs

$1/4$ cup Frangelico

1 tablespoon vanilla extract

1 cup sugar

$1/2$ teaspoon salt

1 quart heavy cream

Cinnamon and nutmeg to taste, optional

Duck

8 duck breasts (5 to 6 ounces *each*)

Salt, pepper and sugar to taste

1 cup olive oil

$1^1/2$ cups Grand Marnier

1 tablespoon sherry vinegar

1 tablespoon sugar

Juice of 3 oranges

3 oranges, peeled and cut into segments

Fresh spinach

Cut each slice of bread in half; brush with melted butter and overlap on the bottom of a 13-inch x 9-inch x 2-inch baking pan. In a bowl, whisk the eggs, Frangelico, vanilla, sugar and salt. Add the cream and mix until thoroughly incorporated. Add cinnamon and nutmeg if desired. Pour over bread; refrigerate for at least 1 hour.

Set the pan inside a larger pan containing at least 1 inch of warm water. Bake at 350° for 1 hour or until fully set. Cool; cut into desired shape.

Score the fat side of each duck breast with a chef's knife. Season with salt, pepper and sugar. In a large sauté pan over high heat, heat the oil. Add the duck, fat side down; reduce heat to medium. Baste the duck with the oil and duck juices for 8–10 minutes. Remove from the heat; add Grand Marnier and let it rest for 5 minutes.

Remove the duck and keep warm. Add sherry, sugar and orange juice to the pan; cook until sauce is reduced. Strain through a fine sieve and return to the heat; add the orange segments. In another pan, wilt the spinach.

To serve, place bread pudding in center of plate; place spinach around it. Slice duck and fan on top of pudding. Cover with sauce and serve.

The Strater Hotel

The future of Durango had yet to be determined when Henry Strater, a Cleveland pharmacist, had the faith it would prosper. The city would need a hotel—and he wanted to be the one to build it. He had no hotel experience, but he had enthusiasm, and with the help of his father and brothers, the Strater Hotel opened in 1887.

It cost $70,000 to build the four-story hotel, with 376,000 native red bricks and hard-carved sandstone cornices and sills. Each room boasted its own wood-burning stove and comfortable furniture. Outside was a three-story privy, with strategically placed holes.

The Strater was just one sign of progress beginning to appear in Durango in the late 1880s and early 1890s ... there was an electric trolley, a three-story skyscraper with an electric elevator (Newman Building at 800 Main) and electric lights with a home-owned electric company.

Durango itself was the child of the Denver & Rio Grande Western Railroad Company, established in 1879. Company management laid out the charming downtown that remains today, though when the railroad first arrived in town on August 5, 1881, Durango was dubbed the new City in the Wilderness or Smelter City, as it was host to the region's growing smelting, mining and agricultural economy.

With the then state-of-the-art rail transportation and the quick money made by the miners, enterprising merchants,

ranchers and farmers settled into the valley, giving a balance to the city's economy and culture. The newcomers built churches, schools and many of the fine buildings and Victorian homes still standing today. The growing business district on Main Avenue helped Durango fulfill its self-proclaimed destiny as the business capital of the region.

Strater had located his own pharmacy in the prominent corner of his hotel, which he leased to H.L. Rice, not intending to run the property himself. Under Rice's management, the Strater became known as the place of social gathering.

Being inexperienced in business, Strater had neglected to exclude his pharmacy location in the lease to Rice. Rice charged a high rent, which infuriated the young pharmacist and prompted him in 1893 to build the competing Columbian Hotel directly to the south. The hotels competed toe to toe until 1895, when the silver panic put them both out of business.

The Bank of Cleveland repossessed the Strater and sold it to Ms. Hattie Mashburn and Charles E. Stilwell. Stilwell took the hotel through the turn of the century and developed a more refined appeal by offering such things as opera and fine dinners.

A few noted personages have made the Strater their home away from home. Western author Louis L'Amour always asked for the room directly above the Diamond Belle Saloon, Room 222. He said the "honky-tonk music" helped set the mood for his novels of the Old West. Indeed, he wrote a

The Strater Hotel

699 Main Avenue

Durango, Colorado 81301

(970) 247-4431

(800) 247-4431

www.strater.com

good portion of his Sackett novels at the Strater.

During the Roaring '20s, Durango's economy chugged along. Oil and gas had been discovered, and coal still fired the narrow-gauge railroad. In 1926, a group of Durango businessmen, lead by banker Earl A. Barker Sr., formed an organization to buy the now aging hotel, and the group focused on refreshing the image of the 39-year-old property.

In 1954, Barker's son, Earl Jr., and his wife, Jentra, began another renovation, giving special attention to air-conditioning, heating, bathrooms and real closets. They are the ones who started the hotel's collection of American Victorian-era walnut furniture, which has grown into the largest of its kind in the world today.

While attending a hotel convention in Atlanta, the couple spotted an authentic Victorian bed in an antique store, giving them the idea to use period furniture in some of the rooms. They cashed in their airline tickets and drove from Georgia to Colorado, pulling a trailer and stopping at antique stores along the way. Their finds created a true Victorian charm in the hotel's décor.

Since 1983, Rod Barker has carried on his parents' tradition, overseeing installation of fine woodwork and beautiful hand-stenciled wallpapers. Windowed showcases brimming with antique collectibles are located throughout the public areas, inviting guests to explore the history of Durango and the Strater Hotel. Each of the 93 guestrooms is now individually and uniquely designed (and the Victorian beds have been updated to standard sizes, including some queen and king).

With the help of master woodworker Charles Schumacher, Rod designed and remodeled the hotel lobby and added the stunning new Office Spiritorium, which has become a favorite spot for relaxing in lush, turn-of-the-century surroundings while enjoying coffee or "spirits."

Durango is surrounded by some of the most breathtaking mountain scenery in the world. The narrow-gauge railroad is still in operation, chugging between Durango and Silverton. Plus, some of the most spectacular and well-preserved Puebloan ruins in the United States are found within a 100-mile radius of the Strater Hotel. Mesa Verde National Park, Chaco Canyon, the Aztec Ruins and Salmon Ruins are fascinating places to visit to learn about the ancestral Puebloan culture, which predates Durango's history by at least 1,300 years.

GORGONZOLA SALAD
WITH RUSTIN'S RASPBERRY VINAIGRETTE

Serves 4–5

Vinaigrette

1 1/2 pints fresh raspberries (frozen raspberries may be substituted)

3/4 cup raspberry wine vinegar

3/4 cup fresh basil

1/2 cup sugar

1/3 cup finely diced red onion

1/2 teaspoon oregano

1 1/2 teaspoons granulated garlic

1 1/2 teaspoons salt

3/4 teaspoon white pepper

Dash Worcestershire sauce

3 cups olive oil

1/2 cup water

Garlic Crostini

1/4 cup olive oil, *divided*

8 to 10 slices French bread baguette

2 tablespoons garlic

1 tablespoon minced parsley

1 tablespoon minced basil

Salt and pepper to taste

2 tablespoons grated Parmesan cheese

Salad

1/2 head romaine, torn

1/2 head green leaf lettuce, torn

3 cups mixed baby greens

Pinch salt

1 1/2 cups red grapes, halved

1/2 cup walnuts, toasted

6 ounces Gorgonzola

1 small tomato, diced

1 tablespoon chopped parsley

Chop the raspberries and place in a bowl. Add vinegar, basil, sugar, onion, oregano, garlic, salt, white pepper and Worcestershire sauce. Marinate for 10 minutes. While constantly whisking, add oil and water. Adjust seasoning as needed. Chill for at least 2 hours.

For crostini, brush a baking sheet with olive oil, just enough to coat. Place bread on baking sheet. Mix remaining olive oil and garlic; spoon onto bread. Sprinkle with parsley, basil, salt, pepper and Parmesan cheese. Bake at 325° until crisp.

In a large chilled metal bowl, toss the greens and salt. Strain chilled vinaigrette and pour desired amount over greens; toss to coat. Divide among salad plates. Scatter grape halves, toasted walnuts and Gorgonzola over salads; top each with two pieces of garlic crostini. Sprinkle tomato and parsley on edges of plates.

The Wort Hotel

The Wort Hotel

Glenwood & Broadway

P.O. Box 69

Jackson, Wyoming 83001

(307) 733-2190

(800) 322-2727

www.worthotel.com

From homesteader to hotel owner, Charles J. Wort realized his dream when he built the Wort Hotel in 1941. He and his wife, Luella, first came to Jackson Hole, Wyoming in 1893. They lived in South Park country and had two sons, John in 1900 and Jess in 1903.

In 1915, Wort bought four lots of land in what is now downtown Jackson, a community nestled in the mountain basin known collectively as Jackson Hole. For a number of years, the land was used as a horse corral. From 1932 to 1940, the family operated an establishment that is now Signal Mountain Lodge. After much consideration, they began construction on their dream—a luxury hotel in downtown Jackson. It cost approximately $90,000 to build.

A visit to the Wort wouldn't be complete without stopping in at the Silver Dollar Bar, which was added in 1950, to see what else—the silver dollars! A German cabinetmaker designed and built the distinctive bar, and he inlaid 2,032 uncirculated silver dollars from the Federal Reserve in Denver into it.

Gambling was offered at the Wort until the late 1950s. Although gambling has always been illegal in Wyoming, it was tolerated for years in resort areas as a tourist amusement.

The historic landmark was threatened by one of the worst fires in Jackson history. A bird's nest too close to a transformer started the blaze on August 5, 1980. Locals watched in horror as flames leaped from the hotel roof. The fire burned into the night and caused the roof to collapse. Only days after the fire, a sign went up saying, "We will be back." After much effort and expense, the Wort reopened in June 1981.

The hotel celebrated its 60th birthday in September 2001. Since the beginning, the Wort has been a favorite spot for locals as well as visitors to Jackson Hole. With a prime location near Yellowstone and Grand Teton National Parks, the area is known for its abundance of great year-round activities and adventures.

Listed on the National Register of Historic Places, the Wort has received numerous awards. It's been named one of America's top 50 ski resorts by *Condé Nast Traveler* and one of the country's greatest inns by *National Geographic Traveler*.

The Silver Dollar Grill, which was restored in 2005, offers a true Western dining experience. Come and find out why people say, "Meet me at the Wort!"

COCONUT-PRETZEL CRUSTED SHRIMP
WITH RUM DIJON SAUCE

The dipping sauce is served cold and can be made up to 1 week in advance.

Serves 3–4

1 cup coarsely chopped pretzels

1 cup coconut

1 cup panko (Japanese) bread crumbs

3 eggs

$^1/_2$ cup water

1 cup all-purpose flour

Salt and pepper

12 jumbo shrimp, peeled, deveined and butterflied

Rum Dijon Sauce

3 ounces Malibu rum

3 ounces rice vinegar

2 ounces coconut extract

1 cup Dijon mustard

1 tablespoon sugar

1 tablespoon honey

In a bowl, combine the pretzels, coconut and bread crumbs; set aside. In another bowl, beat the eggs and water. Place flour in a third bowl; season with salt and pepper.

Toss shrimp in flour mixture until well coated; place in the egg wash for 1–2 minutes. Drain the shrimp in a colander for about 2 minutes. One at a time, place shrimp in the pretzel mixture and press the coating into the shrimp. Pan-fry or deep-fry the shrimp until golden brown, about 3–4 minutes.

In a bowl, whisk the sauce ingredients. Season to taste with salt and pepper. Serve with shrimp.

IRISH BREAD PUDDING

Serves 12

6 eggs

1 can (14 ounces) sweetened condensed milk

1 can (12 ounces) evaporated milk

$1^3/_4$ cups whole milk

1 cup sugar

$^3/_4$ cup raisins

$^3/_4$ cup Irish whiskey

2 tablespoons vanilla extract

1 tablespoon cinnamon

1 loaf bread, cubed and lightly toasted

In a large bowl, combine the first nine ingredients; mix well. Add bread cubes and toss thoroughly. Pour into a well-greased 13-inch x 9-inch baking pan. Bake at 350° for 30–35 minutes.

RED CURRANT GRAND MARNIER SAUCE

Makes 2 quarts

4 tablespoons brown sugar

1 tablespoon ground mustard

1 teaspoon ground ginger

1 teaspoon ground cloves

6 cups port wine

2 cups dried currants

2 cups currant jelly

2 cups orange juice

4 tablespoons lemon juice

3 tablespoons orange zest

Cornstarch slurry

$1/2$ cup Grand Marnier

In a saucepan, combine the first 10 ingredients. Bring to a boil. Reduce heat; simmer until reduced by one-quarter. Thicken lightly with the cornstarch slurry and finish with the Grand Marnier.

THE WEST

California, Nevada, Oregon and Washington. The Rocky Mountains and Pacific Coast dominate the West. Tourists flock to Hollywood, Disneyland, Hoover Dam, Sequoia National Forest, California's Sutter's Mill (site of the 1848 gold rush), the Golden Gate Bridge, Lake Tahoe, Las Vegas, Mount Rainier, the Cascade Mountains and Mount St. Helens. This region not only has the largest population but also attracts the most tourists.

The Culinary Institute of America at Greystone

The Culinary Institute of

America at Greystone

2555 Main Street

St. Helena, California 94574

(707) 967-1010

www.ciachef.edu/california

Food and wine enhance one another ... and one of the best places to experience that commingling is the Culinary Institute of America at Greystone, situated in the heart of the acclaimed wine country of California's Napa Valley.

Dedicated to continuing education and career development programs in the fields of food, wine and hospitality, the Culinary Institute is located on the grounds of the former Greystone Cellars winery.

When it was completed in 1889, Greystone was the largest stone winery in the world. A cooperative winery serving upper Napa Valley grape growers, it had a planned capacity of 2 million gallons. The 117,000-square-foot facility, with 22-inch-thick walls of locally quarried tufa stone, was designed by Hammond McIntyre, whose other winery designs in the valley include Trefethen, Inglenook (now Niebaum Coppola) and Far Niente.

From the time of the phylloxera epidemic in the vineyards at the close of the 19th century through Prohibition, Greystone was virtually dormant. In 1950, Christian Brothers, a Catholic lay teaching order, purchased the property to increase production of their well-known brands of wines, brandies and ports under the direction of Brother Timothy, whose world-famous corkscrew collection of more than 1,000 items is on display.

The Greystone facility and the exclusive marketing rights to the Christian Brothers' brands were acquired in 1990 by Heublein Inc., an international food and beverage distributor. The acquisition was concluded just after the Loma Prieta earthquake, which severely damaged the northern portion of the building. Heublein generously sold the building and a nearby 15-acre Merlot vineyard to the Culinary Institute of America (CIA) for about 10 percent of its $14 million value in 1993.

The CIA completed a $15 million renovation of the building and opened for classes in 1995. Some of the unique features preserved during the renovation include the stars on the outside walls (an early attempt at seismic management); the huge redwood entrance doors; the gold leaf Christian Brothers signature; 2,000-gallon redwood casks (filled with water to prevent them from drying out); and the original Christian Brothers' barrel-making display.

Greystone Cellars building, the heart of the campus, houses teaching kitchens and bakeshops, the Rudd Center for Professional Wine Studies, Ecolab Theatre, Spice Islands Marketplace, De Baun Museum, Ken and Grace De Baun Café and the Wine Spectator Greystone Restaurant.

Greystone hosts public cooking demonstrations, special events, seminars and travel programs. Visitors to the campus can dine at the restaurant and shop at the marketplace for cookware, bakeware, culinary tools and specialty food products. It's a fun vacation stop for food and wine lovers alike.

PESTO-STUFFED CHICKEN BREASTS
WITH TOMATO RELISH

Pesto is a paste usually made from garlic, oil, pine nuts, basil and Parmesan cheese. Rich in flavor, it adds an exciting twist to simple chicken breasts. Served with a touch of tomato relish, you have a winner.

Serves 6

Tomato Relish

4 plum tomatoes, seeded and chopped

1 tablespoon extra virgin olive oil

2 teaspoons balsamic vinegar

$^1/_4$ teaspoon salt *or* to taste

$^1/_8$ teaspoon freshly ground black pepper
   or to taste

Pesto

3 cloves garlic, peeled

2 cups packed fresh basil

Juice and zest of 1 lemon

5 tablespoons pine nuts, toasted

$^2/_3$ cup grated Parmesan cheese

1 teaspoon salt *or* to taste, *divided*

$^1/_2$ teaspoon freshly ground black pepper
   or to taste, *divided*

$^1/_4$ cup extra virgin olive oil

2$^1/_4$ pounds boneless skinless chicken breasts

2 tablespoons vegetable oil

In a small bowl, combine the tomato relish ingredients. Cover and refrigerate until chilled.

For pesto, in a food processor, combine the garlic, basil, lemon juice and zest, pine nuts, Parmesan cheese, ¼ teaspoon salt and a pinch of pepper; pulse until finely chopped. Add olive oil in a thin stream until fully incorporated and a thick paste forms.

Place chicken breasts, skinned side down, between two sheets of waxed paper; pound to ¼-inch thickness with a meat mallet. Remove and discard top sheet of waxed paper. Spread each chicken breast with about 2 tablespoons pesto. Starting with the narrower end, roll chicken around the filling; discard waxed paper. Tie chicken with butcher's twine or secure with wooden toothpicks to prevent it from unrolling. Season with remaining salt and pepper.

Heat vegetable oil in a large sauté pan over medium-high heat. Sauté the chicken until golden brown on all sides, about 8–10 minutes.

Place chicken on a baking sheet coated with nonstick cooking spray. Finish in a 400° oven, about 10–15 minutes. Let stand for 5 minutes. Discard string or toothpicks. Slice each chicken breast on the bias into four pieces; arrange on individual plates. Garnish with tomato relish.

MIXED BEAN AND GRAIN SALAD

Serves 8

¹/₂ pound bulgur

³/₄ teaspoon salt *or* to taste, *divided*

3 ounces Israeli couscous

¹/₂ pound green lentils

2 tablespoons red wine vinegar

¹/₄ teaspoon freshly ground black pepper *or* to taste

¹/₄ cup olive oil

¹/₂ cup minced fresh parsley

¹/₂ pound canned chickpeas, rinsed and drained

4 sun-dried tomatoes, minced

8 parsley leaves for garnish

Bring about 3 cups of water to a boil. Measure the bulgur in a large bowl; pour the boiling water over it and let stand until softened, about 15 minutes. Meanwhile, in a saucepan, bring another 3 cups of water to a boil. Add ¼ teaspoon salt and couscous; cook until tender, about 10–12 minutes. Drain and rinse couscous with cold water until cool. Drain bulgur well.

Place the lentils in a medium pot and cover with water. Bring to a simmer; cook for 20 minutes or until tender. Drain and reserve.

In a salad bowl, combine the vinegar, pepper and remaining salt; whisk in oil and add minced parsley. Add the bulgur, couscous, lentils, chickpeas and sun-dried tomatoes; toss until evenly dressed. The salad can be served now or chilled for 15–20 minutes before serving. Use a 4-ounce ramekin or other small bowl to mold the salad, making an elegant presentation. Garnish with parsley leaves.

This healthy salad is chock-full of grains and legumes that not only offer a delicious complement to a variety of entrées, but make nutrition-conscious food fun to eat.

The Davenport Hotel

The Davenport Hotel

10 South Post Street

Spokane, Washington 99201

(509) 455-8888

(800) 899-1482

www.thedavenporthotel.com

The summer of 1889 was fateful for Spokane and for 20-year-old Lewellyn "Louis" Davenport. He'd come to Spokane Falls, Washington Territory, to work in his uncle's "Pride of Spokane Restaurant." In August, a blaze turned 32 square blocks into ashes. Davenport salvaged what he could, bought a tent and opened "Davenport's Waffle Foundry." From this humble beginning, Davenport created a hospitality empire that became famous around the world.

After the fire, Spokane rebuilt quickly. Washington became a state that winter, and Spokane dropped the "Falls" from its name. With timber, mining, agriculture and the railroad pouring money and people into the region, Spokane was poised to become one of the great cities of the West.

Recognizing his opportunity, Davenport leased a brick building on the northeast corner of Sprague Avenue and Post Street and expanded his culinary offerings to nearly 100 items. Business was so good, Davenport bought an adjoining building and in 1904 hired up-and-coming architect Kirtland Cutter to make the two buildings appear as one. The Mission Revival-style white stucco walls and red tile roofs stood in marked contrast to every other building downtown.

The Davenport Hotel was neither Louis Davenport's idea, nor was it built with his money. Leading businessmen desired a large public house for boarding and entertaining guests. They wanted a building to speak for the ages, as architecture does, that Spokane was built by great men. Great men were sought to build and run it, and their search for the best men of architecture and hospitality ended with their first choices, Cutter and Davenport.

With the leverage of Davenport's already strong name, the Davenport Hotel Company was formed in 1912. The hotel tower went up in eight months of 1913 using horse carts, steam jacks and hand tools. Not a single worker was seriously injured or killed—a rarity for the time.

Cutter and Davenport shopped the world for ideas and furnishings ... Cutter designed spaces inspired by the great architects of France, England and Spain. Davenport filled them with fine art and prepared to seat his guests at tables dressed in the finest Irish linens from Liddell and set with 15,000 pieces of silver (the largest private commission ever created by Reed & Barton).

Ever since opening day in September of 1914, the hotel has promoted itself as "one of America's exceptional hotels." It was the first hotel with air-conditioning, a central vacuum system, housekeeping carts (designed by Davenport himself) and accordion ballroom doors. The Spokane newspaper introduced the hotel to the public with a special Sunday insert trumpeting "the new $2 million hostelry of Spokane," even though the project was 50% over budget and actually cost $3 million.

The Davenport Hotel was the largest private telephone branch exchange in the Pacific Northwest (with 450 handsets) and was also the largest and most complicated plumbing job (with 30 miles of pipes delivering hot, cold and drinking water to every one of its 405 rooms). Gilded with gold, sparkling with crystal and illuminated throughout with "electroliers" (chandeliers), it was as grand as the finest ocean liners of the day.

Hotel Monthly, in September 1915, described Louis Davenport as "the man with a vision who created a hotel with a soul." He demanded perfection in every facet of his operation. He ordered silverware be set exactly one thumb-knuckle from the edge of the table ... coins be washed and bills be pressed through housekeeping before being given in change ... and the lobby fireplace be always burning as an abiding symbol of hospitality.

When his hotel was called "the house of comfort," Davenport was extremely pleased. He wrote, "In all things, the hotel sincerely tries to so well please its guests that they will be glad they came, sorry to leave and eager to return."

Many of those guests were famous—royalty, captains of industry, stars of stage and screen and just about every American president of the 20th century. In these halls, you can walk in the shadows of Charles Lindbergh, Amelia Earhart, Mary Pickford, Clark Gable, John Philip Sousa, Lawrence Welk, Marian Anderson, Bob Hope and Benny Goodman, to name just a

few. Authors Zane Grey and Dashiell Hammett wrote scenes in their works set at this most famous hotel in the West. A selection of archive photos and artifacts in display cases makes for an enjoyable stroll along the hotel's mezzanine.

The Davenport was home to the first commercially licensed radio station in Spokane—KHQ, which signed on the air in 1922. KHQ featured many local bands, including The Musicaladers. That group's drummer dropped out of Gonzaga University and became world famous for his singing voice. His name was Harry "Bing" Crosby.

Davenport sold his beloved hotel in 1945 and saw it die around him. He passed away in his suite in 1951. Each successive owner took more than they gave to the property, and it was closed in 1985. It remained so until March 2000, when local entrepreneurs Walt and Karen Worthy bought the entire city block for $6.5 million.

The couple spent the next two years of their lives—and $38 million of their own money—to make the Davenport grand again. Public spaces and ballrooms were restored to what they would have looked like when new. The guest floors were taken back to bare concrete and built anew with fresh wiring, plumbing, drywall, furniture and fixtures. In September 2002, the ringing of a ship's bell eight times signaled a change of the watch—and the Davenport Hotel reopened as a perfect blend of old and new.

OYSTER STEW

Serves 8–10

¹/₄ pound red bell peppers, finely diced

¹/₄ pound fresh asparagus, trimmed and chopped

1¹/₂ teaspoons minced garlic

2 tablespoons clarified butter

¹/₃ cup Worcestershire sauce

5 shakes Tabasco

2 quarts extra-small oysters

1 quart heavy whipping cream

Salt, pepper and additional Worcestershire sauce and Tabasco to taste

¹/₄ cup chopped green onions *or* chives

In a soup pot, sweat the red peppers, asparagus and garlic in butter. Add Worcestershire, Tabasco and oysters. Cook until reduced by one-third. Add heavy cream. Bring to a boil; reduce by another third. Add salt, pepper, and additional Worcestershire and Tabasco to taste. Garnish with chopped green onions or chives.

CHOCOLATE MOUSSE

Makes 8 cups

20 ounces semisweet chocolate, chopped

¹/₂ cup egg yolks

¹/₄ cup sugar

¹/₂ cup honey

4¹/₂ cups heavy whipping cream

Melt the chocolate over a double boiler. Meanwhile, in a mixing bowl, whip egg yolks and sugar. Heat honey in a pan over medium-high. In another bowl, begin whipping cream to soft peaks. When yolks and sugar reach pale-yellow ribbon stage, slowly add simmering honey. Add melted chocolate; blend until smooth. Add a fourth of the whipped cream and blend until smooth. Carefully fold in remaining cream. Spoon into dessert dishes.

RED WINE BUTTER SAUCE

Makes 1 cup

1 cup red wine

2 shallots, roughly chopped

1 teaspoon cracked black pepper

2 tablespoons heavy whipping cream

1 cup unsalted butter, cubed, room temperature

Salt to taste

In a saucepan, combine the wine, shallots and pepper. Cook over medium heat until reduced to ¼ cup. Add cream and reduce for 2 more minutes. Remove from the heat; slowly whisk in the butter, a little at a time, until all of the butter is incorporated. Season with salt. Strain and keep warm until serving.

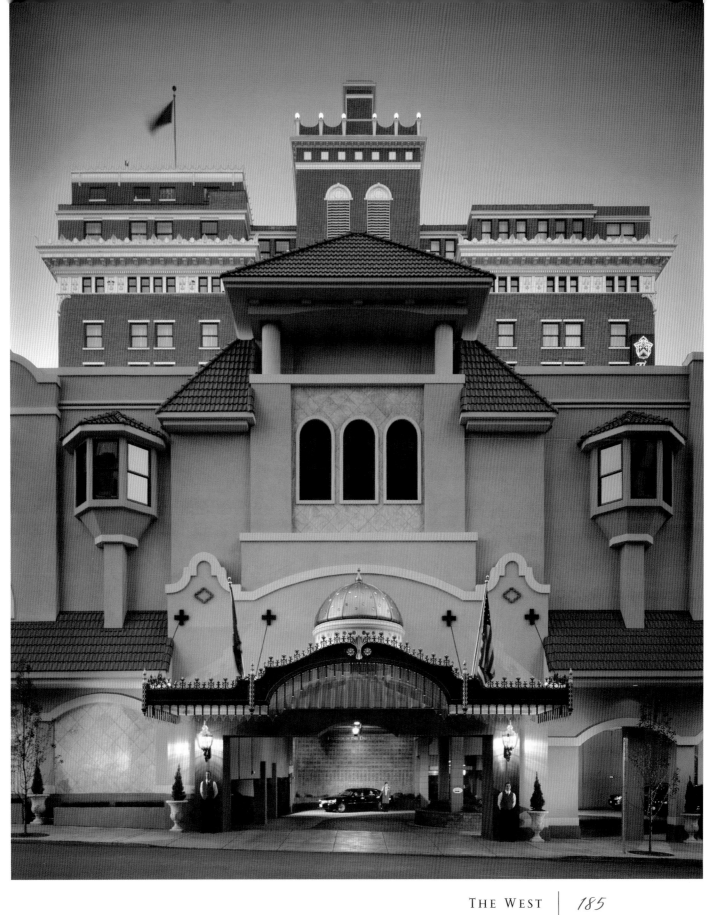

Hotel del Coronado

Hotel del Coronado

1500 Orange Avenue

Coronado, California 92118

(619) 435-6611

www.hoteldel.com

It started with a dream. In 1888, California's picturesque Coronado peninsula, a stone's throw from the developing city of San Diego, showed its promise to Elisha Babcock and Hampton Story, who wanted to build a hotel that would be "the talk of the western world."

The 1848 discovery of gold in northern California had attracted a substantial population to the West, but much of the nation's interior was still wild nearly 40 years later when Babcock and Story came to Coronado to hunt. They purchased the peninsula for $110,000 and proceeded to subdivide it into lots, then auctioned off the lots in a single day and made enough profit to build a magnificent hotel.

Construction costs were $600,000, and furnishings cost another $400,000. At the time, Hotel del Coronado was one of the largest buildings in the country to offer electric lights, telephones and elevators. Another modern convenience was running hot and cold water. Hot and cold running seawater was also offered. Fine china and linens came from Europe, while carpets and furniture came from the East, along with many of the original employees.

The Del was promoted as a hunting and fishing resort, so the chef was kept busy cooking the guests' catch of the day. Activities included bowling, croquet, swimming, boating, bicycling, archery and golf; there were separate billiard rooms for men and women, as well as rooms set aside for chess, cards, reading, writing, smoking and music.

Tired of the usual resorts, sophisticated travelers from the East flocked to the Del. A few of the wealthiest arrived in their own railcars. Since some guests stayed for months at a time, a school was opened.

Son of "Sugar King" Claus Spreckels, John D. Spreckels purchased the Del and moved his family there from San Francisco after the earthquake of 1906. While leading the hotel during the Gilded Age, he was also responsible for helping modernize San Diego. He built a streetcar system, published two newspapers, developed real estate, ran a water company and built his own railroad line.

After Spreckels' death in 1926, his family continued to own the hotel, but the Depression and war took its toll. During WWII, many Navy pilots were housed at the Del, even though the hotel remained open for the few tourists and businessmen who visited. Military weddings and honeymoons were common fare. In 1948, the family sold the Del, and it passed through several owners before its recent $55 million renovation.

Renowned for its magnificent architecture, Hotel del Coronado is equally well known for its legendary guests. Ten United States presidents have stayed at the resort, starting with Benjamin Harrison in 1891.

Aviator Charles Lindbergh was honored at the hotel after transatlantic flight. Thomas Edison visited during 1915, and legendary sports figures Babe Ruth, Jack Dempsey, Willie Mays, Magic Johnson and Muhammad Ali have all been guests.

In 1920, England's Prince of Wales visited the Del. Wallis Spencer Simpson was living in Coronado at the time, and people have speculated that may have been when the two met. Edward would go on to become King, but in 1936, he gave up the throne to marry Mrs. Simpson, who was divorced.

With its proximity to Los Angeles, Hotel del Coronado has attracted movie stars since 1901, when the first film was made in Coronado. The long list includes Rudolph Valentino, W.C. Fields, Douglas Fairbanks Sr., Charlie Chaplin, Mary Pickford, Al Jolson, Greta Garbo, Mae West, Rita Hayworth and Clark Gable. In 1958, *Some Like It Hot,* starring Marilyn Monroe, Jack Lemmon and Tony Curtis, was filmed at the Del. Television stars Carol Burnett, Donna Reed, Raymond Burr, Doris Day and Dinah Shore were among the regular guests.

One guest who arrived in 1892 has reportedly never left! According to legend, Kate Morgan checked into the hotel, brokenhearted and alone, in November of that year. Five days later, she was found dead on the beach, a gunshot wound to her head. Apparently, Kate had killed herself after a quarrel with her estranged husband. Since that time, resort guests, employees and even paranormal researchers have attested to the fact that the room Kate stayed in is haunted by her spirit.

Even more intriguing is stepping into the world-famous Crown Room, the original dining room built in 1888. Whimsical crown-shaped chandeliers, designed by *Wizard of Oz* author L. Frank Baum (another frequent guest), drop from the glowing sugar-pine ceiling. Spacious windows circling the room offer spectacular views. The Crown Room was the site of the largest State Dinner held outside the White House—Richard Nixon gave the dinner in 1970 in honor of Mexican President Gustavo Diaz Ordaz.

Today, the Crown Room is the Del's premier dining facility, offering an award-winning Sunday brunch, special events and holiday celebrations.

DEBBIE REYNOLDS'
FRESH FRUIT FANTASY
WITH PECAN-YOGURT DRESSING

Debbie Reynolds and Donald O'Connor performed at the Del's centennial weekend celebration. They sang and danced their way to a standing ovation from the 700 guests. Before her performance, Ms. Reynolds chose the Fresh Fruit Fantasy for dinner.

Serves 1
Pecan-Yogurt Dressing
1 cup plain yogurt
1 tablespoon honey
2 teaspoons lemon juice
¼ cup finely chopped pecans
Fruit Salad
¼ fresh papaya
¼ cantaloupe
1-inch slice seedless watermelon
3 slices pineapple
¼ plum, pitted and sliced fan-style
1 fresh blueberry
4 sections pink grapefruit
3 sections orange
1 kiwifruit, peeled and cut into 3 slices
6 fresh raspberries
Fresh mint sprigs

In a small mixing bowl, combine the dressing ingredients and blend thoroughly.

Transfer to a small serving bowl; cover and refrigerate for at least 2 hours or overnight.

Peel and seed the papaya and cantaloupe. Cut the fruit into parallel slices lengthwise, leaving intact at the base fan-style. Cut watermelon slice into quarters and place in the center of the plate. Arrange papaya fan on the right side of watermelon; arrange cantaloupe fan on the left side. Place pineapple slices over watermelon, below the papaya and cantaloupe. Place plum fan on top of pineapple and blueberry at the base of the plum.

Arrange grapefruit sections next to the watermelon. Place the orange sections above watermelon. Place kiwi slices down the center of the plate; place two raspberries on each kiwi slice. Garnish with sprigs of mint placed at the 3, 6, 9 and 12 o'clock positions. Serve with desired amount of pecan-yogurt dressing.

"A good cook is like a sorceress who dispenses happiness."
– Elsa Schiaparelli

The Fairmont San Francisco

The Fairmont San Francisco

950 Mason Street

San Francisco, California
   94108

(415) 772-5000

(800) 257-7544

www.fairmont.com/
   sanfrancisco

A symbol of survival, the Fairmont San Francisco hadn't yet opened when the great earthquake struck the city in 1906, but it rose to great heights in the rebuilding afterward. The hotel was completed, and interior furnishings had just been delivered prior to the tragic events of April 6.

The story actually begins in 1902. Tessie and Virginia Fair were building the Fairmont as a grand monument to their late father, James Graham Fair, one of San Francisco's wealthiest citizens who'd struck it rich in a Nevada silver mine. By 1906, the construction had become too much of a burden for the sisters. They sold it to Herbert and Hartland Law in exchange for two existing office buildings at Mission and New Montgomery streets. How could anyone have known a devastating earthquake was just days away?

Photographs taken at the time show the Fairmont standing proudly at the top of Nob Hill, surrounded by devastation and rubble. It had withstood the quake, with some interior structural damage, but it couldn't escape the uncontrollable fires, which reached the top of the hill 24 hours later.

The Law brothers went ahead with plans to repair, redecorate and, where necessary, restore. They hired Julia Morgan, the first woman graduate of the prestigious Ecole des Beaux Arts in Paris.

Exactly a year after the earthquake, the Fairmont celebrated its grand opening with a banquet, where 13,000 oysters, 600 pounds of turtle and $5,000 worth of California and French wines were served.

The Fairmont quickly became the social hub of the City. Wealthy families, displaced by the earthquake, took up residence. The Laws had signed a 10-year deal for the Palace Hotel company to manage the hotel, but then Tessie (Fair) Oelrichs returned to her beloved city after her husband passed away. By May 1908, she was again the owner and hostess par excellence.

D.M. Linnard, who had a chain of hotels in California, took over the management in 1917, and in '24 he bought the controlling interest from the Oelrichs family. In 1929, he sold the Fairmont to George Smith, a mining engineer, who had just completed the Mark Hopkins Hotel. Smith undertook a major renovation, including adding an indoor pool, the "Fairmont Plunge."

In the '40s, the hotel was suffering from neglect, but it "rose from the ashes" yet again. Benjamin Swig, an East Coast businessman, purchased the Fairmont and hired Dorothy Draper, the most famous decorator of the time, to transform the lobby and public areas. Her goal was to restore the Fairmont to its position as the center jewel in the crown of San Francisco's Golden Age. Her design innovations—black and red carpets, wild geranium and strawberry colors, gold and black lacquer— replicated a flamboyant atmosphere synonymous with the California Gold Rush.

The Fairmont was once again the place to see and be seen. Meanwhile, the hotel had made news with its role as the venue for the International Conference, which led to the birth of the United Nations. The plaque commemorating the drafting of the U.N. Charter can still be seen outside the Garden Room, while the flags of the original signatories fly proudly above the porte cochere.

The Venetian Room also benefited from the "Draper touch." From its grand reopening in 1947 all the way through the '80s, it was San Francisco's premier supper club. Guests and locals dined and danced to big-name entertainment: Ella Fitzgerald, Nat "King" Cole, Marlene Dietrich, Joel Grey, Bobby Short, Vic Damone, James Brown and many more. The Venetian Room is most famous as the place where Tony Bennett first sang "I Left My Heart in San Francisco."

Another exciting venue was the *S.S. Tonga*—the former "Fairmont Plunge" pool was given a makeover, with a "shipshape" atmosphere, exotic drinks and Chinese food. The *S.S. Tonga* went into dry-dock and was replaced by the current Tonga Room, where patrons can relax under tiki huts, sip a mai tai, dine from a South Seas menu and dance on the gleaming dance floor.

Guests can also enjoy the Laurel Court, which has been restored to its original design and once again functions as the hotel's main dining room. The bountiful produce, local ingredients and great wines of Northern California are featured prominently on the menu.

For over 40 years, the Fairmont has promised the most beautiful views of the city from its Crown Room at the top of the 23-story Tower, which was designed by Mario Gaidano and opened in 1961. To get to the top, visitors ride San Francisco's first glass elevator. Richard Swig, Ben's son, supervised every phase of construction, ensuring the quality met Fairmont standards. The Fair sisters would have approved.

A story about the Fairmont wouldn't be complete without mention of the fabled Penthouse—its most exclusive (and at $10,000 per night, its most expensive) accommodation.

John S. Drum, president of the American Trust Company, designed and constructed the residence for himself in 1926. Arthur Upham Pope, a noted professor at UC Berkeley and expert on Persian Art, decorated the interior. The rotunda of the two-story library, which depicts the constellations of the nighttime sky, and the "map room" bedroom were decorated by artist Robert Boardman Howard.

The Penthouse was later to become home to another VIP, Benjamin Swig. Chief Justice Earl Warren, Governor Pat Brown and General Omar Bradley were a few of the luminaries who shared his hospitality. After Swig passed away, the Penthouse was a home away from home for celebrities and dignitaries.

As the San Francisco residence for every U.S. president since William Taft, the Fairmont garnered a world-class reputation, and the list of grand hotels bearing its name grew. In 1999, Fairmont Hotels merged with Canadian Pacific Hotels to form Fairmont Hotels & Resorts, the largest operator of luxury hotels and resorts in North America.

The company's flagship, the Fairmont San Francisco greeted the 21st century with an award-winning $85 million restoration.

AHI TUNA TARTARE AND SMOKED SALMON ON RICE PAPER
WITH GINGER, WASABI CRÈME FRAÎCHE AND CRISP NORI

Serves 6

1 teaspoon cornstarch

3 sheets nori seaweed, cut into 6 large triangles

6 Vietnamese rice paper wrappers

2 ounces wasabi powder

¼ cup crème fraîche

1¼ pounds sushi grade #1 ahi tuna

¼ cup pickled pink ginger, julienned

2 ounces sesame oil

1 bunch shiso (Japanese mint), chopped

12 ounces smoked salmon

1 package daikon sprouts

1 bunch chervil

Mix cornstarch with water; coat the nori just before frying. Fry in neutral oil at 375°. Also fry the rice paper wrappers ahead of time; shape into small cups. Both will keep for 2 days in a covered dry container.

Mix the wasabi powder with 1 tablespoon of water, then whisk into crème fraîche; set aside. Dice the tuna into ½-inch cubes, removing any white threads. Place in a small metal bowl. Just before serving, mix in the ginger, sesame oil, shiso and pinch of black pepper.

To serve, plate 2 ounces smoked salmon on each plate; drizzle with wasabi mixture. Place rice paper cup on top; fill with 3 ounces of tuna mixture. Garnish with daikon, chervil and crispy nori.

"After a good dinner, one can forgive anyone, even one's own relatives."

—Oscar Wilde

The Governor Hotel

In the prosperous days following the Lewis and Clark Exposition, the Governor Hotel (originally known as the Seward Hotel) was built in 1909. Held in Portland in 1905, the Exposition commemorated Meriwether Lewis and William Clark's journey from Missouri to the Pacific Northwest in 1804–1806. This significant event is featured prominently today in the hotel, where guests can get a "history lesson" while staying at the Governor.

In the old lobby, a massive four-panel mural traces the expedition—depicting a map of the journey ... American Indians fishing for salmon at Celilo Falls on the Columbia River ... Lewis trading with the Nez Perce Indians ... and a dramatic, windswept image of Sacajawea, Lewis and Clark's Indian guide, looking across the Oregon coast to the Pacific Ocean. The contemporary work was created by San Francisco artist Melinda Morey.

Another notable piece of art, an 8-foot stained-glass dome, has been part of the hotel since it opened and was possibly designed by the architect himself. When the hotel was closed for a time, a carpet store occupied the ground-floor space.

When that business relocated, the dome was dismantled and stored in its warehouse. During renovations, the dome was carefully repaired and placed in its original location, over what had been the hotel's reading room. Below the dome is the original floor tile, a pattern that has been carried throughout the entry and restaurant.

The hotel's original architect, William C. Knighton, was known for incorporating a bell theme into his designs, and many of these bells can still be spotted throughout the building. The older hotel is connected internally to the Princeton Building, which was built in 1923 for the Portland Elks Lodge, the local chapter of the national fraternal organization.

Now known as the West Wing, the building's ceremonial rooms, public spaces and athletic clubs underwent a major renovation in 1984. A great deal of the original Italian Renaissance décor is still visible, particularly in the appropriately named Renaissance Room and Grand Ballroom on the third floor.

The second floor of the Princeton houses several function rooms for events and meetings. Highlighting an array of amazing craftsmanship, the rooms are named for how they were used by the Elks Club: the Vault Room, formerly the business office, still has two bank teller-style windows and a sealed vault door ... the Fireside Room, decorated to reflect details shown in historic photos, has angels on the domed ceiling and Corinthian columns along two walls ... the Library is paneled in black walnut and, of course, has books on the shelves ... and the Billiard Room is richly painted in bold black, red and olive, with birds of paradise and winged cobras in its décor. The Card Room is the least ornate, because its true treasure is hidden from view—the inlaid tile floor features every card in the deck but is

The Governor Hotel

614 SW 11th Avenue

Portland, Oregon 97205

(503) 224-3400

(800) 554-3456

www.govhotel.com

securely protected from wear by specially installed carpeting.

The original hotel did not have a kitchen or dining facilities of any sort. The space now occupied by Jake's Grill restaurant and kitchen was the hotel lobby and guest lounge.

The Grand Heritage Hotel Group acquired the Governor in late 2003 and wanted to refresh the spirit of this Portland monument. Renovation, which began in summer 2004, included moving the lobby to the West Wing, adding a guest elevator for the East Wing and reopening the 7,500-square-foot Heritage Ballroom. The designers succeeded in beautifully blending the classic character of the hotel with a warm, modern appeal.

CRAB AND SHRIMP LOUIE

Serves 1

4 ounces Oregon Bay shrimp

2 ounces Dungeness crab

1/2 head iceberg lettuce

6 cucumber slices (1/4 inch thick)

6 black olives, pitted

1 hard-cooked egg, halved

4 wedges vine-ripe tomato

1/2 cup Thousand Island dressing

2 parsley sprigs

1 lemon wedge

Cook the shrimp and crab; refrigerate until chilled. Just before serving, finely slice the lettuce and place in the middle of the plate. Arrange cucumber slices around the lettuce; place an olive on each slice. Place an egg half on each side of lettuce, with tomato wedges next to eggs. Drizzle with dressing. Top with shrimp and crab. Garnish with parsley and lemon.

STRAWBERRY AND ARUGULA SALAD

Goat Cheese Roulade

8 ounces goat cheese

1/4 clove garlic, finely minced

1 tablespoon olive oil

Salt and pepper to taste

Sherry Vinaigrette

3 tablespoons sherry vinegar

3 tablespoons champagne vinegar

5 ounces olive oil

5 ounces salad oil

1/2 teaspoon honey

For each serving

6 fresh strawberries

1 1/2 ounces arugula

Salt and pepper to taste

In a mixing bowl, whip the goat cheese until loose and malleable. Add the garlic, olive oil, salt and pepper. Spread onto plastic wrap and roll into a cylinder about 1¾ inches in diameter. Refrigerate for 2 hours.

In another bowl, whisk the vinaigrette ingredients. Slice and fan three strawberries; quarter the remaining strawberries. Place the fanned strawberries in three different points on the serving plate. Toss the quartered strawberries and arugula with 1 tablespoon sherry vinaigrette; season with salt and pepper. Place the salad in the center of the plate in three small handfuls to create as much height as possible. Place a slice of goat cheese roulade against the salad.

Millennium Biltmore Hotel Los Angeles

Millennium Biltmore Hotel

Los Angeles

506 South Grand Avenue

Los Angeles, California 90071

(213) 624-1011

(800) 245-8673

www.millenniumhotels.com

With its grand architecture and impressive guest list, the Millennium Biltmore Hotel opened as the "Host of the Coast" on October 1, 1923 and remains so to this day.

The architecture features the opulent style of the Spanish-Italian Renaissance to reflect the Castilian heritage of California. Detailed ceiling frescoes depicting mythological themes were executed by "modern-day Michelangelo" Giovanni Battista Smeraldi, whose work also graces the White House and the Vatican. Accenting these fresco murals are wall reliefs, sculpted columns and bronze work.

Legends and traditions thrive within the embellished walls of the Biltmore, as it has played host to the people and events contributing to the history of Los Angeles. From Cary Grant to Brad Pitt, countless movie stars have passed through its doors. As a testament to the role that the Biltmore has played in Hollywood, the monumental decision to found the Academy of Motion Picture Arts and Sciences was made in the hotel's own Crystal Ballroom, with many of its corresponding Oscar awards ceremonies taking place in the Biltmore Bowl.

In addition to its connection with the Hollywood film industry, the Biltmore has also welcomed public figures such as John F. Kennedy and the Duke and Duchess of York to enjoy its beautiful facilities. The significant events that have taken place at the hotel, and the succession of important people who have experienced its welcoming hospitality, is as impressive and unparalleled as the majestic architecture of the hotel itself.

A downtown Los Angeles landmark since its completion, and the "star" of numerous movies and TV shows filmed at the property, the Millennium Biltmore has long been the meeting spot for high society, celebrities and conventioneers from around the globe.

The stately 683-room property celebrated a landmark 80th anniversary by bringing back jazz to its grand Gallery Bar, hosting a daily high tea in the Rendezvous Court and establishing a "Historic Corridor" for guests to relive its colorful history.

The Crystal Ballroom and 14,000-square-foot Biltmore Bowl, site of the early Academy of Motion Picture Arts and Sciences banquets, recently reopened after a $3 million renovation to prepare the grand venue for another century of memorable events. The hotel also features three restaurants, including Sai Sai, which serves authentic Japanese cuisine.

PASTA FRIJOLES

Serves 20–24

3 ounces olive oil

1¹/₂ ounces fresh garlic

¹/₄ ounce fresh basil

¹/₄ teaspoon crushed red chili peppers

1¹/₂ teaspoons minced fresh thyme

1 large yellow onion, chopped

1³/₄ pounds Roma tomatoes, chopped

¹/₂ cup white wine

1 quart chicken stock

³/₄ cup diced celery

³/₄ cup diced carrots

1 bay leaf

1 ounce dry cavatappi pasta

12 ounces cannellini beans, cooked

Salt and pepper to taste

Heat up a large pan. Add olive oil, garlic, basil, chilies and thyme; cook for a few seconds. Add onion and tomatoes; cook until dissolved. Deglaze pan with wine until it evaporates.

Add chicken stock, celery, carrots and bay leaf. Bring to a boil. Add pasta; cook until al dente. Add cooked beans. Season with salt and pepper. Remove bay leaf before serving.

KAKI SHISHITO

This appetizer features pan-fried oysters on the half shell with Japanese green peppers and tomato yuzu salsa. Yuzu and kaiso can be found in Japanese markets.

Serves 2

12 live oysters on the half shell

All-purpose flour

Oil for frying

12 shishito (Japanese green peppers)

Kaiso (fresh Japanese seaweed)

Tomato Yuzu Salsa

1 cup cherry tomatoes, chopped

¹/₂ cup finely chopped white onion

¹/₄ bunch cilantro, chopped

1 jalapeño, seeded and chopped

¹/₂ teaspoon chopped fresh garlic

6 tablespoons yuzu (Japanese citrus) *or*
   juice of 3 lemons

Reserve oyster shells for serving. Dust oysters with flour and pan-fry in a little oil until one side is golden and crisp; turn and leave for 10 seconds in hot pan (you just want to cook one side of the oyster). Pan-fry the shishito. Combine the salsa ingredients. Place seaweed on the oyster shell; top with an oyster, crispy side up. Top with a spoonful of salsa and garnish with a shishito.

DUNGENESS CRAB GAZPACHO

Serves 4–6

Cilantro Oil

1 bunch cilantro with stems

2 cups olive oil, *divided*

Gazpacho

5 ripe tomatoes

2 medium cucumbers, peeled, seeded and diced

$\frac{1}{2}$ medium red onion, diced

2 jalapeños, diced

$\frac{1}{2}$ cup chopped cilantro

2 ounces champagne vinegar

1 to 2 limes

Salt and pepper to taste

Crabmeat (1 ounce for each serving)

Fresh cilantro leaves for garnish

In boiling water, blanch cilantro for 15 seconds, then plunge in an ice-water bath. Drain and pat dry. Place cilantro in a blender; add ½ cup olive oil. Purée for 30 seconds. Pour into a stainless steel container. Add the remaining oil; let stand overnight. Strain through a coffee filter.

Peel tomatoes and place in a strainer. Over a bowl, squeeze out seeds and juice; discard the seeds. Purée half of the tomatoes and dice the remainder. In a large nonreactive container, combine the tomatoes, cucumbers, onion, jalapeños, chopped cilantro, vinegar and juice from 1 lime. (Juice from a second lime is optional.) Refrigerate overnight. Season with salt and pepper.

To serve, ladle ¾ cup gazpacho into a dish. Drizzle with 1 teaspoon cilantro oil. Place 1 ounce of crab in center of dish. Garnish with a cilantro leaf.

Napa River Inn

Napa River Inn

500 Main Street

Napa, California 94559

(707) 251-8500

(877) 251-8500

www.napariverinn.com

History abounds at Napa River Inn, starting with its location in the Historic Napa Mill. The inn's primary structure is the Hatt Building, which is the cornerstone of the mill and was built in 1884. It was named after Captain Albert Hatt, the original owner and visionary who created a thriving business along the Napa River.

Hailing from Germany, Hatt was called "Captain" since he had been sailing since the age of 14. He gave up the sea to build this property.

At the time, the river was the primary means of transportation, and many businesses were located along its shores. Situated in the middle of all this activity, the Napa Mill enjoyed a booming business.

Not only did the building serve as a warehouse, but it also offered recreation— the White Rock maple floor upstairs served as a roller-skating rink. A silo was added in 1887 and another building was constructed later to house machinery for grain processing.

Sadly, Albert Hatt Jr. did not enjoy the same success his father did. In poor health and burdened with five children and business problems, Albert Jr. hung himself at the age of 46, in 1912, from a beam in the warehouse.

That area is now Sweetie Pies Bakery, where vestiges of the old mill days still exist in the form of an old grain-bagging machine on display. The bakery is a popular morning spot for coffee lovers.

Following Albert's suicide, Robert Keig purchased the Mill from Captain Hatt, and the Keig family continued to operate the Napa Mill Feed Store until 1974. More recently, both Albert Hatt and Robert Keig have been the subject of ghost stories. One of these accounts involves a woman who looks to be Albert's wife walking the halls of the inn at night. On other occasions, inn guests have reported talking to a man who insisted that the building was not a modern hotel, but rather a mill building, and then he disappeared. They later identified the man as Robert Keig from an old photo hanging in the hotel.

The modern Napa River Inn features oversized quarters with fireplaces, canopy beds, tufted lounge chairs, velvet ottomans, slipper tubs and walk-in showers. In keeping with the historic restoration, rooms have maple hardwood floors, and massive cove and baseboard moldings.

Art in the Hatt Building rooms reflects a burgeoning river town of the 1800s. Hatt Hall's interior appointments include the original pressed-tin wall panels and deep cove moldings, originally installed in the space when it was a music room in the late 1800s.

Preservation efforts began in 1990, when Harry Price undertook his vision to restore and transform the dilapidated and abandoned warehouse property into an entertainment complex. The Historic Napa Mill project is the largest historic redevelopment undertaking in the history of Napa.

BRAISED LAMB SHANKS
WITH WINTER ROOT VEGETABLES

Serves 4

4 lamb shanks (1 pound *each*)
1 ounce all-purpose flour
Salt and pepper
3 large carrots, chopped
2 large red onions, chopped
2 heads garlic, broken into cloves (unpeeled)
1 bunch fresh thyme
2 bay leaves
1 gallon Cabernet
$\frac{1}{2}$ gallon veal stock
$\frac{1}{4}$ pound baby turnips, peeled
$\frac{1}{4}$ pound baby carrots
2 ounces slab bacon, diced
$\frac{1}{2}$ pound celery root, peeled and diced
4 tablespoons grapeseed oil

Dust lamb shanks with flour; season with salt and pepper. In a large pot or Dutch oven, pan-sear until golden brown. Remove lamb. Add carrots, onions, garlic, thyme and bay leaves; roast until vegetables are tender. Deglaze pan with wine; cook until reduced by half. Add stock. Bring to a boil. Season with salt and pepper. Return lamb shanks to the pan. Cover and braise for 2½ hours or until meat is very tender.

Meanwhile, cook the turnips and baby carrots separately, with water, sugar, butter, salt and pepper on high heat, until water has evaporated and vegetables are tender; set aside. Blanch bacon in cold water for 1 minute; drain. Sauté until crispy; set aside. Sauté celery root in grapeseed oil until lightly tender.

Before serving, combine all vegetables with bacon. Check seasoning. Add a small amount of butter and 1 tablespoon of water so mixture does not get dry. Spoon vegetable mixture onto serving plates; top each with a braised lamb shank. Pour braising juices over the meat and vegetables. Place a sprig of chervil on the lamb shank. Serve hot.

CHOCOLATE CHUNK COOKIES
WITH DRIED SOUR CHERRIES

2 1/2 cups rolled oats

2 cups all-purpose flour

1 teaspoon baking powder

1 teaspoon baking soda

1/2 teaspoon salt

1/2 pound unsalted butter, room temperature

1 cup packed brown sugar

1 cup sugar

2 eggs

1 teaspoon vanilla extract

1/2 cup dried sour cherries

2/3 cup chopped walnuts

6 ounces bittersweet chocolate chunks

Combine the oats, flour, baking powder, baking soda and salt; set aside. In an electric mixer with the paddle attachment, cream the butter and sugars until smooth but not light. Scrape the bowl. Add the eggs, one at a time, scraping after each addition (batter will look curdled). Add the dry ingredients in two additions, scraping after each. Do not overmix. Combine the cherries, walnuts and chocolate; add to the dough just until incorporated. Chill for 1–2 hours.

Scoop the dough onto a parchment-lined baking sheet. If the dough is cold, press down slightly. Bake at 350° for 10 minutes. Turn the pan and continue baking for 7–12 minutes. The cookies will be brown on the edges, but the center will still be on the lighter side. Cool on wire racks.

Note: Cookie dough may be shaped into balls and refrigerated or frozen for future use.

Index

Acknowledgments

First and foremost, we want to thank our publisher, Rue Judd, whose energy, insight and professionalism led to the completion of this book. We embraced the same desire to preserve history, share recipes and provide travelers with fascinating destinations to explore.

We also want to thank the staffs of all the hotels, inns and restaurants—who shared the vision of a project of this magnitude— and especially the chefs, who graciously provided invaluable support and tasty dishes to please the palate.

Historic preservation is a concept close to our hearts, and travelers who choose to visit these properties will be delighted with the food, the ambience and the hospitality they encounter. And to each reader, thank you for embarking on this American culinary odyssey.

PHOTO CAPTIONS

Photographs on pages 72–75 are courtesy of The Colonial Williamsburg Foundation. Photographs on pages 13, 18–21 and 190–193 are courtesy of Fairmont Hotels. Remaining photographs are courtesy of the pictured establishment.